D0074781

THE
HISTORY OF
MYANMAR

THE HISTORY OF MYANMAR

William J. Topich and Keith A. Leitich

The Greenwood Histories of the Modern Nations
Frank W. Thackeray and John E. Findling, Series Editors

GREENWOOD

AN IMPRINT OF ABC-CLIO, LLC
Santa Barbara, California • Denver, Colorado • Oxford, England

Library of Congress Cataloging-in-Publication Data

Topich, William J.
     The history of Myanmar / William J. Topich and Keith A. Leitich.
          p. cm. — (The Greenwood histories of the modern nations)
     Includes bibliographical references and index.
     ISBN 978-0-313-35724-4 (hardcopy: alk. paper) — ISBN 978-0-313-35725-1 (ebook)
1. Burma—History.   I. Leitich, Keith A.   II. Title.   III. Series: Greenwood
histories of the modern nations.
     DS528.5.T67   2013
     959.1—dc23   2012029072

ISBN: 978-0-313-35724-4
EISBN: 978-0-313-35725-1

17   16   15   14   13   1   2   3   4   5

This book is also available on the World Wide Web as an eBook.
Visit www.abc-clio.com for details.

Greenwood
An Imprint of ABC-CLIO, LLC

ABC-CLIO, LLC
130 Cremona Drive, P.O. Box 1911
Santa Barbara, California 93116-1911

This book is printed on acid-free paper ∞

Manufactured in the United States of America

Contents

Series Foreword

The Greenwood Histories of the Modern Nations series is intended to provide students and interested laypeople with up-to-date, concise, and analytical histories of many of the nations of the contemporary world. Not since the 1960s has there been a systematic attempt to publish a series of national histories, and as series editors, we believe that this series will prove to be a valuable contribution to our understanding of other countries in our increasingly interdependent world.

Some 40 years ago, at the end of the 1960s, the Cold War was an accepted reality of global politics. The process of decolonization was still in progress, the idea of a unified Europe with a single currency was unheard of, the United States was mired in a war in Vietnam, and the economic boom in Asia was still years in the future. Richard Nixon was president of the United States, Mao Tse-tung (not yet Mao Zedong) ruled China, Leonid Brezhnev guided the Soviet Union, and Harold Wilson was prime minister of the United Kingdom. Authoritarian dictators still controlled most of Latin America, the Middle East was reeling in the wake of the Six-Day War, and Shah Mohammad Reza Pahlavi was at the height of his power in Iran.

Since then, the Cold War has ended, the Soviet Union has vanished, leaving 15 independent republics in its wake, the advent of the computer age has radically transformed global communications, the rising demand for oil makes the Middle East still a dangerous flashpoint, and the rise of new economic powers such as the People's Republic of China and India threatens to bring about a new world order. All of these developments have had a dramatic impact on the recent history of every nation of the world.

For this series, which was launched in 1998, we first selected nations whose political, economic, and sociocultural affairs marked them as among the most important of our time. For each nation, we found an author who was recognized as a specialist in the history of that nation. These authors worked cooperatively with us and with Greenwood Press to produce volumes that reflected current research on their nations and that are interesting and informative to their readers. In the first decade of the series, more than 40 volumes were published, and as of 2008, some are moving into second editions.

The success of the series has encouraged us to broaden our scope to include additional nations, whose histories have had significant effects on their regions, if not on the entire world. In addition, geopolitical changes have elevated other nations into positions of greater importance in world affairs and, so, we have chosen to include them in this series as well. The importance of a series such as this cannot be underestimated. As a superpower whose influence is felt all over the world, the United States can claim a "special" relationship with almost every other nation. Yet many Americans know very little about the histories of nations with which the United States relates. How did they get to be the way they are? What kind of political systems have evolved there? What kind of influence do they have on their own regions? What are the dominant political, religious, and cultural forces that move their leaders? These and many other questions are answered in the volumes of this series.

The authors who contribute to this series write comprehensive histories of their nations, dating back, in some instances, to prehistoric times. Each of them, however, has devoted a significant portion of their book to events of the past 40 years because the modern era has contributed the most to contemporary issues that have an impact on U.S. policy. Authors make every effort to be as up-to-date as possible so that readers can benefit from discussion and analysis of recent events.

In addition to the historical narrative, each volume contains an introductory chapter giving an overview of that country's geography, political institutions, economic structure, and cultural attributes. This is meant to give readers a snapshot of the nation as it exists in the contemporary world. Each history also includes supplementary information following the narrative, which may include a timeline that represents a succinct chronology of the nation's historical evolution, biographical sketches of the nation's most important historical figures, and a glossary of important terms or concepts that are usually expressed in a foreign language. Finally, each author prepares a comprehensive bibliography for readers who wish to pursue the subject further.

Readers of these volumes will find them fascinating and well written. More importantly, they will come away with a better understanding of the contemporary world and the nations that comprise it. As series editors, we hope that this series will contribute to a heightened sense of global understanding as we move through the early years of the 21st century.

Frank W. Thackeray and John E. Findling
Indiana University Southeast

Acknowledgments

We would like to thank numerous people for their help in the research and editing of this book, including Pulaski Academy for their continued help and support, and the library staff at the University of Arkansas at Little Rock. In addition, we would like to mention the staff at the National Archives, especially Ashby Crowder. Nicole Topich-Young assisted in the editing of the manuscript on numerous occasions. Professors Ross Marlay and Charles Hartwig were outstanding mentors and piqued our interest in Southeast Asian Studies and International Affairs during our time in graduate school at Arkansas State University. We must acknowledge our indebtedness to Louise Macfarlane at the Imperial War Museum, San San May, Curator, Burmese Section at British Library, Paul Rascoe, PCL Reference—Documents, Maps, Electronic Info Librarian at the University of Texas, and Lynne M. Thomas, Curator, Rare Books and Special Collections at Northern Illinois University, who kindly offered their services in helping to locate source material for this book.

Our editor at ABC-CLIO, Kaitlin Ciarmiello, was patient throughout the entire process and we could not have finished the manuscript without her guidance and support.

Finally, Bill would like to thank his wife, LaDonna, and their daughters Nicole and Kristin. They were all very supportive and had to endure Bill's extended time away during the research and writing stages. Keith would like to express his heartfelt thanks to his wife, Jamilya, for her sympathetic understanding, unwavering support, and seemingly boundless patience. He would also like to thank his daughter, Olivia, who always brings a smile to her dad's face.

Timeline of Historical Events

5000–3000 BCE	The Anyathian culture flourishes in northern Burma.
500 BCE	The Pyū enter the upper portion of the Ayeyarwaddy valley.
300 BCE	The Mon begin settling in the Sittang valley.
100 BCE	The Pyū arrive in Burma and establish the city-states of Beikthano, Mongamo, Śrī Kṣetra, Peikhonomyo, and Halingyi.
656	Śrī Kṣetra is abandoned.
832	The Tai-Shans of Nan-Chao conquer the Pyū capital of Halingyi.
900	The Burman arrive in northern Burma.
1057	King Anawrahta conquers Thaton and founds the first unified Burmese state at Bagan.
1277	The Bagan army advances into Yunnan to confront Kublai Khan's Mongol army.

1287	Bagan king Narathihapati is assassinated by his son Thihathu.
	Following King Narathihapati's assassination, the Mongol army defeats the Bagan army at the battle of Bagan.
1364	The Burman Ava dynasty is founded at Inwa in northern Burma.
1369	The Mons transfer their capital to Bago.
1385–1425	War between Inwa and Bago.
1433	Mrauk-U is founded.
1436–1449	The kingdom of Ava fights a series of campaigns against the Min and the Tai in Yunnan that later become known as the Luchuan-Pingmian campaigns.
1486	King Min-gyi-nyo founds the first Toungoo dynasty at Toungoo.
1519	The Portuguese establish a trading station at Martaban.
1527	The Shan overrun the kingdom of Ava.
1531	The Toungoo dynasty reunites Burma.
1539	The Toungoo dynasty invades Muang Chiang Kran.
1560	The Toungoo conquer the city-state of Manipur.
1563	The Toungoo defeat Ayutthaya, the capital of Siam, and force Ayutthaya to pay tribute.
1597	The Nyaunggan dynasty or Restored Toungoo dynasty is founded.
1613	Anaukhpetlun defeats the Portuguese.
1614	The Toungoo lay siege and eventually take Chieng Mai.
1687	Captain Weltden lays claim to Negrais Island.
1753	King Alaùngpayà drives Pegu forces out of northern Myanmar.
1755	King Alaùngpayà founds the Konbaung dynasty.
1757	In June, Ensign Robert Lester is sent to Pegu by the British government as "Ambassador Extraordinary."

	In July, Great Britain and Burma sign the Treaty of Friendship and Alliance that grants the East India Company the island of Negrais and a tract of land at Bassein for factories.
1783	Burma recognizes Arakan; a direct frontier is established between Burma and British-administered Bengal (Chittagong). The Naat River is the boundary line.
1824–1826	The Treaty of Yandabo ends first Anglo-Burmese war. Burma cedes suzerainty over Arakan between Chittagong and Cape Negrais to British India. Burma recognizes Manipur, Cachar, and Jaintia as British territories, is compelled to pay Britain an indemnity, and accepts the appointment of the British resident at Ava. Burma agrees to negotiate a commercial treaty with Great Britain.
1852	Outbreak of the second Anglo-Burmese war. Great Britain annexes lower Burma, including Rangoon, Pegu, and Martaban.
1853–1878	An industrial revolution takes place during the reign of King Mindon.
1872	The fifth Buddhist synod is held in Mandalay.
1876	Burma's first ambassador to Europe, Kinwun Mingyee U Kaung, travels to Europe aboard the Yaynanyinthar.
1878	The British dispatch the ship Irrawaddy to Thayetmyo.
1885	Outbreak of the third Anglo-Burmese war. The British capture Mandalay.
1886	Burma becomes a province of British India.
	David Sime Cargill founds the Burma Oil Company (BOC).
1886–1895	The Burmese wage a guerilla war against the British in northern Burma.
1901	Standard Oil Co. begins operations in Burma.
1906	The Young Men's Buddhist Association is founded in Rangoon. This is considered the start of the nationalist movement.
1920	Establishment of the General Council of Burmese Association and the demand for constitutional advancement.

	Students at Rangoon University strike in protest against Burma's exclusion from the Government of India (GOI) Act.
1923	Burma becomes a governor's province under provisions of the GOI Act. Sir S.H. Walter becomes the first governor of Burma.
1930	Formation of the Do Bama Asi Ayon and the radicalization of the nationalist movement.
1930–1932	Hsaya San's peasant rebellion.
1937	Burma is ceded from India and becomes a crown colony. Ba Maw becomes Burma's first prime minister.
1938	Oil field workers' strike.
1939	U Pu becomes prime minister.
	The Communist Party of Burma (CPB) is formed.
1940	U Saw becomes prime minister.
1941	The Burmese Independence Army is formed in Bangkok, Thailand.
1942	The Burmese Independence Army enters Burma.
1942–1945	The Japanese Imperial Army occupies Burma.
1943	The Japanese grant nominal independence to Burma.
1945	The Burma Independence Army initiates an anti-Japanese uprising.
	Britain liberates Burma from the Japanese and reestablishes British administration of Burma.
1947	The Aung San-Attlee Agreement is signed.
	The Panglong Agreement is signed.
	Constituent Assembly elections are held.
	Aung San is assassinated by political opponents.
1948	Burma becomes independent and U Nu becomes the first prime minister of an independent Burma.
	Burma joins the United Nations and becomes its 59th member.

1958–1960	General Ne Win heads a "caretaker government" following a split in the ruling Anti-Fascist People's Freedom League (AFPFL) party.
1960	The AFPFL faction led by U Nu wins parliamentary elections.
1961	U Thant becomes the third United Nations Secretary-General.
1962	A military coup d'état led by General Ne Win removes U Nu from power. He then implements the "Burmese Way to Socialism"—nationalizing the economy, forming a single-party state, and banning independent newspapers.
1974	A new constitution transfers power from the armed forces to a people's assembly headed by the military. U Thant's body is returned to Burma for burial.
1975	Minority groups form the National Democratic Front.
1981	Ne Win gives up the presidency to General San Yu but continues in his role as the chairman of the ruling Socialist Programme Party.
1982	The Burmese citizenship law is passes. The law designates people who are considered nonindigenous as "associate citizens" and denies them rights offered to full citizens.
1983	North Korean agents try to assassinate South Korean President Chun Doo Hwan during his state visit to Burma. The bomb kills 21 South Korean government officials and four Burmese dignitaries as well as wounding 42 but Chun Doo Hwan escaped unharmed.
1987	A currency devaluation triggers massive antigovernment riots.
1988	The border between Burma and China is officially opened. Thousands of demonstrators are killed in antigovernment riots. The State Law and Order Restoration Council (SLORC) is formed. Aung San Suu Kyi cofounds the National League for Democracy (NLD).

1989	SLORC declares martial law, arrests thousands of opposition supporters, and renames Burma as Myanmar. The name of the capital Rangoon is changed to Yangon.
1990	The NLD easily win the elections allowed by the government, but the SLORC invalidates the result.
1991	SLORC decides to extend Aung San Suu Kyi's house arrest by another three years.
	The Nobel Committee awards Aung San Suu Kyi the Nobel Peace Prize.
1992	General Than Shwe replaces General Saw Maung as SLORC chairman, prime minister, and defense minister.
	Several political prisoners are released in an effort to improve Myanmar's international image.
1993	The United States imposes an arms embargo on Myanmar.
1994	A ceasefire agreement is signed between the Kachin Independence Army (KIA) and the government.
1995	Aung San Suu Kyi is released from house arrest after six years.
1996	Aung San Suu Kyi attends the first NLD congress since her release from house arrest.
1997	The United States expands financial sanctions to include all new investments.
	Myanmar is granted admission to the Association of Southeast Asian Nations (ASEAN).
	SLORC renames itself the State Peace and Development Council (SPDC).
1998	The SPDC releases 300 NLD members from prison.
2000	SPDC lifts restrictions on the movements of Aung San Suu Kyi and senior NLD members.
	Aung San Suu Kyi negotiates clandestinely with the SPDC.
2001	The Myanmar army and Shan rebels clash along the Thai border.

2002	General Than Shwe begins construction of the new capital, Naypyidaw, which means "abode of kings," on a remote plain 200 miles north of Yangon.
	Aung San Suu Kyi released from house arrest after a period of 20 months.
2003	Aung San Suu Kyi taken into "protective custody" following clashes between the NLD and the government.
	Khin Nyunt becomes prime minister. He proposes to hold a constitutional convention in 2004 as part of the "road map to democracy."
	U.S. President George W. Bush approves the Burmese Freedom and Democracy Act, which bans the imports of Burmese goods and restricts American banks from doing business in Myanmar.
2004	The government and the Karen National Union agree to a ceasefire.
	The constitutional convention begins in May but is boycotted by the NLD. The convention is adjourned in July.
	Khin Nyunt is removed from his post as prime minister by SPDC chairman Than Shwe amid reports of a power struggle.
	Thousands of political prisoners are released, including leading dissidents of the 1988 pro-democracy student demonstrations.
	The 2004 Indian Ocean tsunami hits Myanmar's coastline reportedly killing 59 people and leaving more than 3,000 homeless.
2005	The NLD and ethnic groups boycott the constitutional convention after its resumption.
	Myanmar turns down the rotating ASEAN chairmanship for 2006.
	The government moves the capital to a site near town of Pyinmana.
2006	Construction of the new capital, Naypyidaw, is completed at the cost of several hundred millions of dollars.

2007   Myanmar and North Korea restore diplomatic ties.

                The government extends Aung San Suu Kyi's house arrest
                for another year.

                The military government declares constitutional talks
                complete and closes the national convention.

                In what is called the Saffron Revolution, Buddhist monks
                lead a series of protests against the government in Yangon
                to protest the deteriorating economic conditions in
                Myanmar. Aung San Suu Kyi meets demonstrating
                monks. The government cracks down on protests, but the
                demonstrations continue.

                SPDC reasserts control over Yangon, arresting thousands
                of Buddhist monks.

                The United Nations General Assembly approves a reso-
                lution condemning the government actions and asks for
                the release of political prisoners.

2008   The SPDC drafts a new constitution and calls for new
                elections in 2010. The new constitution is set for a national
                referendum on May 10.

                Tropical cyclone Nargis hits Myanmar leaving over
                134,000 dead or missing and causing widespread devas-
                tation in the Ayeyarwaddy River delta.

                Tens of millions of dollars in aid are pledged to the survi-
                vors of cyclone Nargis. A total of 78,000 are estimated to
                have died and another 56,000 missing. The government
                estimates economic damages at about US$11 billion.

                The SPDC extends Aung San Suu Kyi's detention by an-
                other year.

                Myanmar's state-run newspaper said the overwhelming
                election victory by Aung San Suu Kyi's party in 1990 has
                been nullified by the approval of a military-backed con-
                stitution and the NLD should prepare for new elections
                in 2010.

2009   Thailand expels hundreds of members of Myanmar's
                Muslim Rohingya minority who appeared off its coast.
                Myanmar denies the Rohingyas' existence.

United Nations envoy Ibrahim Gambari meets with Aung San Suu Kyi.

A UN report said Myanmar faces food shortages because of last year's cyclone.

The NLD offers to take part in elections in exchange for the release of all political prisoners and changes in the constitution.

Aung San Suu Kyi's house arrest is extended for an additional 18 months following a conviction for breaching the terms of her confinement when American John Yettaw swam uninvited to her lakeside residence. Yettaw is sentenced to seven years hard labor but is released when U.S. Senator Jim Webb intervenes on his behalf.

2010   The SPDC announces a new election law that bans political prisoners and monks participation in the forthcoming national elections. The law disqualifies Aung San Suu Kyi from participating due to her previous convictions.

The NLD refuses to participate in the forthcoming elections.

The SPDC announces elections will be held on November 7. The Union Solidarity and Development Party (USDP) wins by a large majority. Opposition and Western observers allege widespread fraud.

Aung San Suu Kyi is released a week after the elections.

2011   Thein Sein is sworn in as president.

The government frees thousands of prisoners under an amnesty.

Aung San Suu Kyi is invited to several meetings with government officials, including President Thein Sein in Naypyidaw.

President Thein Sein lifts restrictions on the media and the Internet. The government passes a law allowing the establishment of trade unions.

A 17-year ceasefire between the Myanmar and the KIA is broken when fighting erupts along the northern border.

The government of Myanmar suspends construction of the $3.6 billion Chinese-funded Myitsone hydroelectric dam on the upper Ayeyarwaddy River in northern Kachin state.

Myanmar agrees to hold the rotating chairmanship of the ASEAN in 2014.

Aung San Suu Kyi says she will stand for a seat in parliament in the Kawhmu constituency in the April 1, 2012, elections as the NLD rejoins the political process.

U.S. Secretary of State Hillary Clinton visits Myanmar. She holds talks with President Thein Sein in the capital of Naypyidaw and meets with Aung San Suu Kyi in Yangon. The visit was the first senior American official to Myanmar in over 50 years.

Myanmar participates in an international landmine ban meeting in Cambodia for the first time.

The government signs a truce with Shan rebels and halts military operations against ethnic Kachin rebels.

2012   British Foreign Secretary William Hague meets with President Thein Sein and other senior government leaders. Mr. Hague also meets with opposition leader Aung San Suu Kyi. The visit is the first by a British foreign secretary since 1955.

Thai Prime Minister Yingluck Shinawatra meets with General Min Aung Hiaing at Government House in Bangkok, Thailand. The meeting aimed at strengthening the two countries' relations.

Australia eases its sanctions on Myanmar by removing some people from a list of Myanmar officials targeted with financial and travel restrictions.

Myanmar's government signs a ceasefire with the Karen National Union, ending one of the world's longest-running ethnic insurgencies.

The United States restores full diplomatic relations with Myanmar hours after the new civilian government released many of its political prisoners including Min Ko Naing and other leaders of the "88-generation students" group, which include Nilar Thein, Htay Kywe, Mya Aye, and the ethnic Shan leader Khun Tun Oo.

French Foreign Minister Alain Juppé visits Myanmar, where he awards Aung San Suu Kyi France's highest honor, the Legion of Honor.

Aung San Suu Kyi registers to run for a parliamentary seat in the Kawhmu constituency in the April 1 by-elections.

The European Union (EU) suspends visa bans on leading politicians from Myanmar.

The NLD wins 43 out of 45 seats in landmark parliamentary by-elections considered to be free and fair by observers. Aung San Suu Kyi wins the seat of Kawhmu, near Yangon.

The United States agrees to ease sanctions against Myanmar, including the relaxation of restrictions on Myanmar officials and on financial transactions and investment.

British Prime Minister David Cameron meets with President Thein Sein in Naypyidaw.

The EU agrees to suspend all sanctions except the military embargo against Myanmar.

South Korean President Lee Myung-bak visits Myanmar. This is the first visit by a South Korean leader since the 1983 North Korean bomb attack in Rangoon that killed 21.

The United States eases sanctions against Myanmar.

Aung San Suu Kyi speaks at the World Economic Forum of East Asia in Bangkok, Thailand. This is her first travel outside Myanmar in 24 years.

Indian Prime Minister Manmohan Singh visits Myanmar. The visit is the first by an Indian prime minister in 25 years.

Aung Sang Suu Kyi is invited to visit France at the invitation of new President Francois Hollande.

Thein Sein meets UN Secretary-General Ban Ki-moon in Naypyidaw.

Deadly clashes erupt between Rakhine Buddhists and Rohingya Muslims in Rakhine state. An estimated

30,000 people are displaced and the government declares a state of emergency.

Aung San Suu Kyi visits Switzerland, Norway, Ireland, Great Britain, and France during a historic 17-day trip. This is the first time in 24 years she has been able to visit Europe.

The government releases about 20 political dissidents as part of a presidential amnesty. Among the released are Ko Aye Aung, Than Zaw, and Pyit Phyo Aung.

Vice President Tin Aung Myint Oo resigns. Mr. Tin was a former general with close ties to the military.

Aung San Suu Kyi attends her first session of parliament as a lawmaker after she won a seat in the April 1 by-election.

U.S. President Barack Obama eases sanctions, allowing American firms to invest in Myanmar. President Thein Sein calls for all Western sanctions to be dropped.

U.S. Secretary of State Hillary Clinton meets Thein Sein at a business forum in Cambodia.

Thai Prime Minister Yingluck Shinawatra and Myanmar President Thein Sein sign several key economic agreements, including a pledge by the Thai government to help the government of Myanmar prepare for the chairmanship of ASEAN.

Myanmar is granted access to the European Union's Generalized System of Preferences, which allows access to European markets without quotas or duties.

Aung San Suu Kyi visits the United States for the first time in two decades and meets President Barack Obama in Washington, D.C.

Aung San Suu Kyi finally receives the U.S. Congressional Gold Medal she was awarded in 2008 when she was under house arrest. Also in attendance was Railways Minister Aung Min representing President Thein Sein.

President Thein Sein visits the United States. This is the first by a Myanmar leader in 46 years.

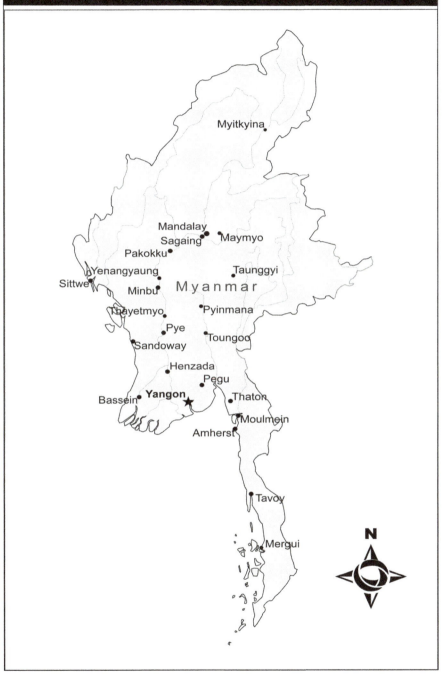

1

Myanmar: An Introduction

GEOGRAPHY

Myanmar is the largest country in mainland Southeast Asia, with approximately 262,000 square miles of territory. Most of the country lies in the latitudes of the tropics, with an abundance of natural resources, fertile land, and plentiful rainfall. Poor agricultural practices along with recurrent natural disasters have created problems for the people of Myanmar. Furthermore, malarial conditions make significant areas of the country uninhabitable. The length of the country stretches over 1,270 miles and it is 580 miles wide at its broadest point. The country borders China on the north and northeast; Laos and Thailand to the east; India and Bangladesh to the northwest; and the Bay of Bengal and the Andaman Sea to the south and west.

Geography impedes national development in Myanmar. The southern part of the country resembles Malaysia, while the north is much more like India or China, and the center falls somewhere in between. With such geographic diversity in land structure, nation building has always been problematic. The first geographic characteristic is the lowland area around the Irrawaddy and Chindwin Rivers. This area is the heartland of Myanmar in which most ethnic Burman and lowlands' groups have lived and worked predominately as rice farmers for most of the past millennium. The second distinctive region consists of rugged mountains and plateaus inhabited by numerous hill tribes. Populations such as the Kachin and Chin would be examples of tribal groups in the mountain areas. The mountains also provide a barrier from potential invasion. The physical separation of the different people has created a sense of disconnect that has historically impeded national unification efforts.

POPULATION AND ETHNICITY

The ethnicity issue in Myanmar has been a constant source of turmoil throughout the history of the region. The term "ethnicity" rather than "tribe" or "nation" can lead to confusion and possible political conflict. Myanmar has approximately 130 different ethnic groups, with their own languages and dialects.

Myanmar is one of the most ethnically diverse countries in the world. The geographical location of Myanmar has caused considerable diffusion from India, China, Thailand, Bangladesh, and Laos. Ethnic minorities constitute over one-third of the entire population of Myanmar.

The most useful way to classify the culture of Myanmar would be along the plain or hill typology. The people of the plains live in the valleys or plains with a complex social and political organization that extends beyond the village. The centers of population are permanent and the main occupation is wet-rice farming. The plains' groups include the Burman (which make up 70% of the total population) along with the Shans, Mons, Arakanese, and delta Karen. The second significant classification would be mountain or hills' people. This hill culture consists of those who live in small units on the slopes or tops of hills, with relative autonomy and a simplistic political structure. Slash-and-burn agriculture would be commonly practiced. Included in this grouping would be Kachins, Chins, and hill Karen.

The largest nonindigenous groups are the Chinese and Indian minorities. Historically, these groups have been a vibrant part of the socioeconomic dynamic of the society. In contemporary times, immigration has been restricted, as the military-led government has drifted toward a more isolationist mindset. It should be noted that Burman refers to the ethnic group, while Burmese refers to the language that Burman people speak, as well as to the citizens of the country. The fact that Burmese is used so extensively in the writings about the country causes confusion at times.

Burman

The Burman (sometimes referred to as the Bamar) are not only the largest ethnic group in Myanmar, but they also have dominated the region historically and politically for the past 1,000 years. The Burman constitute approximately two-thirds of the total population of Myanmar. Many Burman (including several leaders of the country) are from mixed ancestry. It is thus difficult to speak of ethnic homogeneity in Myanmar. Since independence, the Burman have controlled the government and military structure in Myanmar. Minority populations have accused the Burman of attempting to implement a "Burmanization" policy throughout the country. Minority groups claim that they are marginalized in areas such as economics, politics, language, and education. The Burman are overwhelmingly Theravada Buddhist, and this is the main cultural characteristic that defines the group. Educationally, the Bamar language is used in the schools throughout Myanmar.

Karen

The Karens make up the second largest ethnic group in Myanmar. Demographic figures for the Karens range from 2.5 to 7 million. Ethnic Karens live throughout much of Lower Myanmar from the Arakan and delta regions to the Shan state. It is estimated that over 20 Karen subgroups are identifiable.

Many Karens fought with the British army during the colonial period. A sizeable minority of Karens also converted to Christianity by the 20th century. Nationalism among the Karen population has always been strong and friction with the majority Burman has been a constant throughout the history of Myanmar. The most significant obstacle to Karen nationalism has been geography. The Karens are dispersed throughout numerous areas of Myanmar.

Following World War II, Karen aspirations for independence increased. Immediately after the constitutional assembly, Karen militias organized and were bolstered by mass defections of ethnic Karens from the Burmese military, known as the tatmadaw. The Karen National Union was formed in 1949. The Karen movement factionalized along a communist-noncommunist line, which significantly hurt their chances for success.

Chin

The Chin are a Tibeto-Burmese people who reside in the vast mountain chain running up western Myanmar into northeast India. The Chin state borders India and Bangladesh to the west. The Chin lived predominately in the highlands and mostly were involved in labor-intense agriculture. The lack of infrastructure, including the poor quality of roads and communications, along with the poor quality of the land, leaves the population vulnerable at times.

The Chin population is fragmented with over 40 subgroups living in the region. The Myanmar government neglects the Chins. Educational levels are low and economic development in the region is abysmal. The Chin are weary of encroachment from the Myanmar state.

The Chin are noted for their traditional clothing, including intricately woven blankets with elaborate designs. The Chin are also noted for their fascinating tattoos that sometimes cover nearly their entire face. Many Chins converted to Christianity during the British colonial period, and several fought with the British during the World War II.

Kachin

The Kachin are located in northern Myanmar bordering both China and India. The climate in the region inhabited by the Kachin is extreme, with cold winters and oppressively hot summers. By most accounts the most fiercely independent of all ethnic groups in Myanmar, the Kachin's political identity is solid. A well-defined clan system helps to keep the Kachin organized.

The Kachin strongly opposed British colonial efforts, but many were eventually converted to Christianity by the early-20th century. As with the Karen, the Kachin formed a large part of the British colonial army during World War II. The utter devastation of the war led to a strong nationalist movement emerging among the Kachin. During the negotiations for the creation of the 1947 constitution, the Kachin state was recognized with a promise of the right of secession in 10 years. The state boundaries formulated in 1947 fragmented the Kachin population, with a sizable minority placed in the Shan state. Kachin uprisings against the government have been frequent. During 1950 and again in the early 1960s, armed insurrection occurred. In some cases, the upheaval was based on nationalist aspirations; in other cases (U Nu's proclamation making Buddhism the official state religion), the cause was perceived religious intolerance. The Kachin Independence Organization was formed at this time with the stated goal being independence. Throughout the modern history of Myanmar, the Kachin insurgency has been the most formidable enemy of the authorities.

For the most part, the Kachin are rice and sugarcane farmers. The insurgent efforts are also funded by the sale of precious gems on the black market. Furthermore, many Kachin work in the forestry and mining industries. The Kachin are involved in cross-border trading, especially with China.

Kayah

Geographically isolated, the Kayah are located in the very remote mountainous region of the Kayah state. No outside travel is allowed in this particular region of Myanmar. Originally animists, the Kayah were partially converted to Christianity by Baptist and Catholic missionaries. The Kayah are sometimes referred to as "Red Karen" because of their brightly colored clothing. As with the Kachin region, the Kayah were granted autonomy via the

1947 constitution with the right of succession following a 10-year period. The Myanmar military implemented a brutal crackdown against the Kayah insurgents, suppressing nationalist aspirations. The infamous "four cuts" strategy implemented by the military led to humanitarian crisis on numerous occasions. Refugee and internally displaced persons (IDP) problems increased as the tatmadaw incursions into the region accelerated. The Kayah are mostly impoverished subsistence-level farmers. Some economic development comes through mining and hydroelectric plants. A significant minority Kayah population lives in Thailand.

Mon

The Mon civilization is one of the oldest in Southeast Asia. Both Buddhism and writing were introduced to Myanmar by the Mon. Mon independence ended following their defeat at the hands of King Alaùngpayà in the 1750s. What remains of the Mon ethnic group is located in the coastal plains region. Following the upheavals on the late 1950s, Mon nationalism emerged. Discrimination against the Mon persisted throughout the early independence period. The government has attempted to eradicate the use of the Mon language. Mon political parties have been harassed and delegitimized by the authorities. Mon political leaders have been detained and human rights violations against the population are commonplace.

The Mons are more urbanized than most ethnic minority populations. Many Mons end up working in Thai gem mines and many women have been forced into the sex industry. A significant problem for the Mons is their location, which lies in the path of potential natural gas pipelines, as well as their proximity to the gem-mining routes from neighboring Thailand. This unfortunate location problem for the Mon makes them one of the most vulnerable and persecuted ethnic minority groups in Myanmar. The fact that the Myanmar authorities finally recognized a separate Mon state in 1974 did not lessen the tension.

Naga

The Naga population is located in the Putkai range in northern Myanmar. A significant portion of the Naga population resides across the border in India. Many Naga converted to Christianity during the colonial period. The Naga independence movement has been active since the 1950s. Known as fierce warriors, the Naga are renowned for tough resistance against both the tatmadaw as well as the Indian military. The Naga have been denied any formal recognition by the Myanmar authorities. As Indian cooperation with the state of Myanmar increases, the potential threat to the Naga is also accelerating. The constant state of war has caused severe economic hardships to the population.

The future status of the Naga may be more precarious than most of the ethnic minorities of Myanmar.

Rakhines and Rohingya

In many ways, the most volatile situation in Myanmar is in the Arakan territory. The majority Buddhist population known as the Rakhine is in a state of turmoil with the minority Rohingya Muslim minority population. The tension between the groups has increased in recent years.

As with a number of ethnic problems in Myanmar, geography plays a significant role in the heightened tensions. The region lies on the frontier of India and Bangladesh. In the past few years, forced repatriation has increased and significant human rights abuses have been documented. Many of the refugees living in neighboring Bangladesh have been seized, beaten, and forced back into Myanmar. Accusations of anti-Muslim discrimination are commonplace. The Myanmar authorities claim that the Rohingya are not indigenous to the country and are treated as non-citizens.

Shan

The Shan state is the most ethnically diverse region in all of Myanmar. Ten or more ethnic groups constitute a population base of over 100,000, all with different languages and cultural characteristics. Historically, the Shan state included over 40 princely substates who constantly vied for regional control. The internal fighting in the Shan area impeded economic development in the region. At the time of independence, the Shan area was promised the right to secede after the first 10 years. From the time of independence, the Shan area was beset with conflict. From the incursion of Chinese nationalist forces in the 1950s to the separatist movements within Myanmar, the Shan area has remained constantly embroiled in conflict. Further conflict within the region centered on the Communist Party of Burma gaining support from Mao Zedong in the late 1960s. Liberated zones were established numerous times and in places in the Shan area. By the late 1980s, the main source of income for many residents of the Shan state was opium production. The changing global environment complicated the political situation in the Shan region. The Communist Party of Burma lost support and quickly disintegrated. The Shan did participate in the 1990 elections, winning 23 legislative seats. The election results did not halt the fighting within the region. The refugee crisis in the Shan state is overwhelming, with nearly 500,000 IDPs or refugees reported by the late 1990s. Forced conscription of the civilian population is also commonplace. Child soldiers are also forcibly recruited by the tatmadaw. Shan women have also been prey for the sex industry in neighboring Thailand. HIV numbers among the returning women is alarmingly high. Furthermore, numerous members of the tatmadaw from the Shan state mutinied from the government, forming the United Wa State Party.

The Myanmar authorities and the Shan political leaders give radically different numbers regarding the percentage of the population that is part of the Shan state. Nationalist leaders claim the Shan's make up approximately 50 percent of the overall population, while the junta claims the number is closer to one-third.

WOMEN

The status of women in Myanmar has been historically high. Legally, women enjoy rights comparable to men. Women are allowed to own property and can enter any profession. Women have equal inheritance rights with their male siblings and retain control over their dowries. In case of divorce, the wife is entitled to half of the family's assets. Divorce rates are very low in Myanmar. Educational status in Myanmar for women has been impressive. When the university system was fully functional, women made up over half of the college population. Women in Myanmar control most family affairs, and also have a significant role in economic decision making. Women have total access to professional careers such as those in medicine and education.

One of the main areas of contrast would be regarding religion. Particular areas in some of the Buddhists shrines are off limits to females. The birth of a woman is also considered less significant in regard to gaining merit. Over 40,000 women serve as nuns in Myanmar, but that is considered less significant than entering the monkhood. In order to reach the state of nirvana, women must first be reincarnated as males. Finally, the monopoly on power in society by the male-dominated military over the past four decades has helped to reinforce stereotypes of male superiority in Myanmar society.

LANGUAGE

Burmese (part of the Tibeto-Burman languages) is the official language of Myanmar. Burmese is spoken by approximately 80 percent of the population. As with the majority of languages in Southeast Asia, Burmese is a tonal language. Approximately 10 percent of the population speaks Tai languages such as Shan, Khun, and Tai Lu. The Mon of Lower Myanmar and the Palaung of the east speak a Mon-Khmer language. In total, the ethnic minority populations speak over 100 different languages. English is widely spoken in most urban areas.

ECONOMY

Approximately 70 percent of the population of Myanmar is involved in agriculture. The Irrawaddy delta had been one of the most prominent rice growing regions in the world. During the pre–World War II period, substantial migration occurred to the region for employment purposes. The war devastated the economy, as half of the industry and infrastructure was destroyed during the Japanese occupation.

During the postcolonial period, the state of Myanmar was guided by socialist principles. The regimes (both civilian and military) envisioned an economy that was socialist in nature. The upheaval in the early independence period stifled economic development and investment. The Pyidawtha Plan implemented during the time of the Korean War viewed rice exportation as the key to the economic success of Myanmar. Unfortunately, the price of rice plummeted and the plan was never fully enacted.

With state ownership of the land, the peasants lacked sufficient incentives to be fully productive. Furthermore, the cost and scarcity of fertilizer kept profits down considerably. Finally, the lack of infrastructural development has continued to keep Myanmar impoverished.

Myanmar is a resource-rich country that suffers from government mismanagement and immense rural poverty. The main natural resources include teak and other woods, as well as minerals including petroleum, lead, zinc, tin, tungsten, and precious stones, such as jade and sapphires. Myanmar is the largest mainland oil producer in Southeast Asia. The inability to extract natural resources contributes to the economic stagnation in Myanmar. Furthermore, the country has insignificant foreign exchange to purchase machinery and technology to modernize the economy. The overvaluing of the *kyat* leads to inflation and economic imbalances. Several crises in the banking sector have further eroded confidence in the economy system. The connection between the faulting economy and political upheaval has been evident throughout the contemporary period in Myanmar.

Foreign aid is inconsistent due to the massive corruption within Myanmar. Recently, most of the significant aid to Myanmar comes from regional powers China and India, who continue to pursue lucrative concessions from the ruling junta.

RELIGION

The dominant religion throughout Myanmar is Theravada Buddhism. Most significant cultural aspects in Myanmar are tied to Buddhism. Approximately 89 percent of the people in Myanmar are Buddhist. Buddhism entered Myanmar in the 11th century during the reign of King Anawrahta.

The *sangha* (monkhood) have always been deeply respected in society. The religion impacts the society, politics, and economy of Myanmar. Evidence of this is seen by the fact that nearly every village supports at least one monastery or monastic school. Buddhist pagodas dot the landscape throughout the entire country.

The Karen minority of southeast Myanmar practices Christianity, which constitutes four percent of the population. Islam practiced mainly in the Arakanese region also makes up four percent of the population. The remaining percentage is made up of mostly animist beliefs.

GOVERNMENT

Until September 1989, the country of Myanmar was known as Burma. The military junta justified the name change on the grounds that Burma was a vestige of British rule and the harsh colonial past. The United States and Great Britain continue to officially use the name Burma, and many academic journals and books still refer to the country as Burma. Numerous nations and many within the international community, including the United Nations, use Myanmar. In addition to the country name change, most names of cities and geographic locations were altered. For example, Rangoon became Yangon and the Irrawaddy River became the Ayeyarwaddy. Currently the junta calls itself the State Peace and Development Council (SPDC), and it rules Myanmar in an authoritarian fashion.

Myanmar is divided administratively into 14 states. Military commanders in the regions control the political system. Strict authority is maintained by the SPDC, which until recently had a near zero-tolerance policy on political dissent. Censorship, human rights violations, persecution of ethnic and religious minorities, and suppression of individual liberties is commonplace. The position of prime minister is appointed by the SPDC, solidifying the monopolization of power.

The current constitution was last amended in 1974. The junta claims that steps are being taken to fundamentally change the structure and function of the government. A first step in this process was the holding of a referendum in May 2008. This was followed in 2010 by the first democratically held elections in two decades. The process was seriously flawed, with stipulations in place to ensure military dominance over the process and future governing structure.

EDUCATION

Education is required for students age 5 through 10. An examination system is required to qualify for secondary schooling. Less than half of the students in Myanmar qualify for the next level. Even though a significant percentage of students do not advance, literacy rates in Myanmar are nearly 90 percent. Education is thus highly valued in the culture of Myanmar.

Religious institutions, including monasteries, accomplish an essential part of the educational system in Myanmar. Buddhist instruction is emphasized in addition to basic rudimentary skills such as reading, writing, and math. English is widely used in schooling throughout Myanmar. As the junta tries to modernize and integrate with the outside world, the importance of English has become a reality.

2

Prehistory: The Emergence of Civilization in Early Myanmar

The history of Myanmar, formerly known as Burma, dates from prehistoric times to the present. The Mon, the Pyū, and the Arakanese settled throughout Lower Burma, as far as Chao Pya (Menam) valley on the middle branch of the Ayeyarwaddy valley and the Bay of Bengal, respectively, at different times in prehistory. Given the contested historical claims of the origins of the modern Myanmar state and the paucity of written records, much of Myanmar's prehistory is subject to conjecture. What is known about the prehistoric period comes from the limited number of artifacts found and excavations that have been carried out in Myanmar.

The first urban sites began to appear in Upper Myanmar, the Arakan alluvium, and around the Gulf of Martaban. They roughly date from the end of the first millennium BCE and are characterized by burnt brick walls situated near a river. Sometime between 2500 and 1500 BCE, the Mon made their way out of western China, eventually settling between the Thanlwin and Sittang Rivers, becoming the first-known inhabitants of what is now Myanmar. The Mons were not the only inhabitants of Myanmar for long. A few centuries later, a group of tribes that would become known as the Pyū arrived from the Tibetan Plateau. They were followed by the Burman, who would go on to found the first Burmese empire at Bagan.

EARLY HUMAN SETTLEMENT

Although archaeological exploration of one sort or another began in Myanmar over a century ago, our knowledge of the lives of the earliest human inhabitants remain sketchy. The initial Neolithic-age inhabitants of Myanmar were widely dispersed populations of small bands of kin-based communities of hunter-gatherers who migrated from western or central China sometime in prehistory. Archaeological evidence suggests that Myanmar became host to complex cultures and societies sometime around 11,000 BCE. The earliest identifiable human inhabitants of Myanmar were the Paleolithic Anyathian culture, so-named from Anyatha, which is another name for Upper Myanmar. The Anyathian culture dates as far back as 11,000 BCE. The next identifiable human inhabitants bore similarities to the Hoabinhian culture, named for one of the first sites found in Hoa Binh province in neighboring Vietnam, which were characterized by the stone implements found during excavations.

Little is known about Myanmar during the Neolithic period and what is known is poorly understood. The paucity of evidence suggests that these inhabitants were hunter-gatherers as the absence of permanent dwellings indicate the inability to exploit their natural surroundings. Sometime between 11,000 BCE and 5000 BCE, the Anyathian hunter-gatherers transitioned from their relatively mobile existence to a sedentary lifestyle that saw the emergence of wet-rice cultivation in the alluvial valleys of the Chindwin, Ayeyarwaddy, and Thanlwin river systems, where Paleolithic tools have been found. Excavations at the Toungthamon site, located near the 19th-century city of Mandalay, reveal occupation dating from the late Neolithic period to the early Iron Age. Artifacts discovered at Toungthamon show that objects were acquired through trade, indicating affluence, and the specialization of craft production.

Irrigated rice cultivation appears to have begun flourishing in Myanmar by 3000 BCE. Then sometime between 5000 BCE and 2000 BCE, the rice farmers began domesticating cattle and pigs, slowly creating the beginnings of a sedentary agrarian economy. By 1500 BCE–500 BCE, Bronze Age settlements began to appear in the alluvial valleys of Anyatha. The discovery of a Bronze Age cemetery at Nyaunggan, east of the Chindwin River dates occupation to around 1000 BCE and indicates that the production of bronze or the trade in bronze had reached Myanmar by 900 BCE–600 BCE, although with the absence of radiocarbon dating, the date range could be extended to include the period 1500 BCE–100 BCE. The finds at Nyaunggan indicate the existence of a pre–Iron Age culture familiar with skilled stonework and the production of bronze weapons. The finds are also similar to finds in China and Thailand, suggesting a shared material culture or the existence of a vast trade network across prehistoric Southeast Asia.

The first millennium BCE brought about profound social, economic, and political change. Clusters of villages evolved into cities as trade networks created wealth. This, in turn, led to the development of ever more complex societies in Myanmar as agricultural production coupled with the introduction of iron gave rise to urbanization. The first cities emerged independently of each other along the coastline of the Ayeyarwaddy basin in Lower Myanmar and the seasonal tributary rivers of the central plains of Upper Myanmar. The cities were well planned using a combination of indigenous and Indian building techniques. Sacral buildings were constructed using nonperishable materials such as fired brick covered with plaster and sandstone, while secular buildings were built of wood. The use of brick and sandstone in the construction of pagodas and temples was both structural and symbolic. Architecturally, bricks were needed to support and reinforce the pagodas tall cylindrical plinths. By using a structural framing system builders were able to reinforce the framed outer walls. Symbolically, the lavish and massive pagodas and temples reflected both royal piety and temporal power. Timber was used by the general populace because it was both affordable and allowed the construction of buildings according to the various requirements and needs of its owners.

The Mon were the first civilization to emerge in Lower Myanmar. They settled in the Ayeyarwaddy River delta and along the Toninthayi coast. The Mon blended Indian and Mon culture together in a hybrid culture of the two civilizations. The Mon did not remain the sole occupants of Myanmar for long. Another group called the Pyū made their way from the eastern Himalayas of the Tibetan Plateau to the northwestern Ayeyarwaddy valley sometime the first century BCE.

By 300 CE, the Burmans are thought to have made their way to Myanmar from the Tibetan Plateau in northwestern China. By 800 CE, the Burmans had replaced the Pyū as the dominant group in the Ayeyarwaddy River delta and surrounding areas. By the middle of the ninth century CE, the Mons had come to dominate much of Lower Myanmar.

THE ANYATHIAN CULTURE

Myanmar's prehistory begins with the emergence of the Paleolithic Anyathian culture along the Ayeyarwaddy valley in Upper Myanmar. Radiocarbon dating places prehistoric human habitation as far back as 11,000 BCE. Very little is known about the Anyathian culture. What is known comes from the six kinds of hand tools that have been discovered in the 14 archaeological sites along Ayeyarwaddy associated with the Anyathian culture. Additional archaeological evidence suggests the Anyathian were hunter-gatherers who survived by hunting wild animals and foraging wild fruits and vegetables.

The assemblage of stone tools from Anyathian sites bear close resemblance to finds in the Soan site in northeast India and the Choukoutienian sites of China, as well as the Lalmai Hills and Chaklapunji sites in Bangladesh. The technological similarities and distribution of fossil wood assemblages suggest a shared cultural tradition throughout much of Southeast Asia during the pre-historic period. This suggests that there was meaningful contact over a wide area of Southeast Asia that would continue into later historical periods.

Systematic archaeological excavations by the Department of Archaeology, Ministry of Culture, have led to the discovery of cave paintings and stone tools in the Padahlin caves in Ywogen township on the southern Shan plateau. Radiocarbon analysis of the stone tools dates occupation of the caves from 10,000 BCE to 6000 BCE, a period that encompasses both the Paleolithic and the Neolithic periods. The Padahlin caves were the scene of intermittent human habitation for around 4,000 years. The crude pottery shards and stone rings found at Padahlin appear to have been attached to stonecutting tools suggest-ing that they were used for digging. Archaeologists speculate that the tools were probably used to clear patches of forest for cultivation that would indi-cate the shift from hunter-gatherers to cultivated agriculture had begun by the late Neolithic period in Myanmar. As with the polished stone rings found at Ban Lum Khuo and Ban Na Di in Thailand, the stone rings had been drilled with small holes and repaired with bronze wire.

THE EMERGENCE OF THE MON

According to archeologists, the Mon were the first identifiable ethnic group to migrate into what is now Myanmar. Relatively little is known about the origin of the Mon, but it is thought that the Mon began migrating from the Yangtze River valley in southern China to the Upper Mekong as early as 3000 BCE, eventually settling between the Salween and Sittang Rivers in the Ayeyarwaddy River delta and along the Taninthayi coast in Lower Myanmar sometime between 2500 BCE and 1500 BCE. By mid-ninth century BCE, the Mon had come to dominate Lower Myanmar.

According to oral tradition as well as the Indian, Mon, and Burmese chroni-cles, the first Mon kingdom in Myanmar was founded by King Siharaja dur-ing the Buddha's lifetime and was called Suwarnabhumi or "land of gold" and later known as Ramannadesa or "land of Ramanna" located in the lower Ayeyarwaddy River delta near the port of Thaton. Over time the Mon slowly extended their sphere of influence from Cape Negaris in the Ayeyarwaddy delta up to the Chao Phraya delta and into modern Thailand, reaching as far as present-day Laos but were stopped when they encountered the Khmer kingdom at Angkor. There is evidence that the Mon kingdom at Thaton had contact and engaged in trade with both India and Sri Lanka.

Suwarnabhumi is connected with the historical Buddha in later Mon and Burmese chronicles that credit the Mon as the first to establish Buddhism in Myanmar. The Indian, Mon, and Burmese chronicles suggest that the Mon had contact with Buddhism in the third century BCE as Mauryan king Asoká (r. ca. 273–232) is known to have sent a mission of Śrāvakayāna Buddhist monks to Suwarnabhumi where they introduced Theravāda Buddhism to the Mon. Later Burmese chronicles suggest that Buddhist manuscripts from Sri Lanka were translated into Mon characters around 400 CE. Monasteries, stupas, and inscriptions link the Mon in Lower Myanmar with the larger Buddhist community in Southeast Asia.

It appears that from 250 CE to 550 CE the Mon came under nominal control of Funan as the *Liang Shu* (the Annals of the Liang Dynasty) relate how the ruler of Funan utilized Mon troops to attack and conquer neighboring kingdoms. Free of Funanese subjugation, the Mon would go on to found the Dvāravatī Empire, which would last for over 500 years. Major Dvāravatī cities were located at Nakhon Pathom and U-Thong on the plains of Chao Phraya River valley. In 573 CE, the Mon established the kingdom of Hongsavatoi in the area around what is today modern day Pegu. Archaeological excavations reveal the use of extensive irrigation systems in the construction of early Mon cities.

A series of Mon kingdoms continued to exert their influence over much of Lower Myanmar for the next 1,000 years until they came under pressure from the Burman and Tai ethnic groups, who began to assert their growing influence. Even though Princess Camadevi of Lopburi founded the northern Mon kingdom of Haripunjaya in the eighth century CE, Mon power began to the decline and came into conflict with the Burman in the ninth century CE when they founded their own empire around the city of Bagan. Under King Anawrahta (r. ca. 1044–1077), the Burman finally defeated the Mon, capturing and transporting 30,000 prisoners including the Mon king Manuha, the royal family, intellectuals, priests, and craftsmen back to Bagan. In the year 1057 CE, the Burman established the kingdom of Bagan, having defeated the Mon. Although the Mon were defeated militarily, their culture, art, alphabet, writing system, and religion, Theravāda Buddhism, was adopted by Anawrahta. Archaeological evidence points to replacement of Pali and Sanskrit with Mon script in royal documents.

THE ARRIVAL OF THE PYŪ

According to archeologists, the Pyū were the first-known settlers in Upper Myanmar, arriving as far back as 2500 BCE to 2000 BCE. There is archaeological evidence that the Pyū occupied the upper Ayeyarwaddy valley by the first century BCE. Although the origins of the Pyū have been obscured by history, recent archeological evidence suggests that the Pyū were not indigenous to

Myanmar but one of the Tibeto-Burmese tribes that migrated via the eastern Himalayas of Tibet, entering Myanmar along the Salween and Nmai Kha valley, eventually settling in the Ayeyarwaddy valley to the north of the Mon. Over the next couple of centuries, the Pyū spread out into the surrounding areas. The distribution of pre-urban Pyū artifacts suggests that eventually the Pyū settled over a large area across Upper Myanmar.

Archaeological evidence suggests that the Pyū cities developed sometime between 400 BCE and 100 CE when the migrating tribes settled along the seasonal tributary streams of Myanmar's dry zone, which in turn, flow into the Ayeyarwaddy, Sittang, Chindwin, and Mu Rivers. In the second century BCE, clusters of villages slowly evolved into cities that used extensive irrigation systems which created an agricultural surplus that allowed for the specialization of craft production. Archaeological evidence suggests that the city of Beikthano (city of Vishnū) being founded in the first century BCE, and Halingyi shortly thereafter. By the first century CE, the Pyū had established a number of walled cities throughout Upper Myanmar at Beikthano, Mongamo, Śrī Kṣetra, Peikhonomyo, Thayekhettaya, and Halingyi that were ruled as kingdoms. In 167 CE, these cities formed a confederation that they called Pyū.

Pyū political power was concentrated at Śrī Kṣetra, which was at the mouth of the Ayeyarwaddy River. This helped establish Śrī Kṣetra as an alternate trade route from India to China. Prior to the rise of the Pyū, trade passed through northern Myanmar, across the Chindwin River valley to the west. When the mouth of the Ayeyarwaddy River silted up in the eighth century CE, the Pyū moved their capital north to Halin nearer to the trade from India and China.

Excavations undertaken by the Archaeological Survey of Burma suggest that there was a strong Buddhist tradition among the Pyū. Theravāda Buddhism was most likely introduced to the Pyū via overland and maritime trade routes sometime in the first century CE—the writings of Buddhaghosa, Dhammapala, and others start to appear on inscriptions dating to this period. The Pyū slowly began to convert to Buddhism between the first and second century CE as Theravāda monks began emigrating from either southern India or Sri Lanka, introducing Buddhism.

Due to the lack of written material, very little is known about the Pyū themselves. What is known about the Pyū comes from two primary sources: the few stone inscriptions found on burial urns and formulaic inscriptions found in Buddhist votive and accounts recorded in the texts of Chinese court chronicles. Chinese historical sources give the first descriptions of the Pyū. The Pyū were first mentioned in Ch'ang Ch'ü's mid-fourth-century text Hua yang kuo chih. In the Xin Tang shu (New History of the T'ang Dynasty), Sun Laichen gives a detailed description of the Pyū kingdom and its religion, and mentions the eight or nine fortified cities that the Pyū claimed suzerainty over.

Chinese historical records indicate that the Pyū sent tribute missions to the Chinese emperor, accompanied by court dancers and musicians, during the T'ang dynasty (618–906 CE). The last record of the Pyū in Chinese records occurs during the early Song dynasty.

Beikthano flourished from the first to the fourth century CE, while Thayekhettaya flourished from the fourth to eighth centuries CE. Sometime after the fifth century, one of the Pyū tribes, the Burman, began migrating south from present-day Yunnan. The Burman moved south along the Ayeyarwaddy, eventually settling in the fertile plain along the middle course of the Ayeyarwaddy River. Successive invasions slowly weakened the Pyū, thus allowing Burmans to settle in what had previously been Pyū territory. According to Fan Ch'o, author of the *Man-shu,* the kingdom of Nan-Chou in Yunnan attacked and plundered the Pyū capital of Halin around 823–825 CE, enslaving 3,000 Pyū captives and dispersing thousands more into the surrounding areas. Following the invasion by the Nan-Chou the Pyū entered a period of rapid decline in the early ninth century, which the Burman exploited. The Burman filled the post-conflict political vacuum created in the aftermath of Nan-Chou invasions by establishing Bagan as their capital in 849 CE. Pyū language and culture seem to have been slowly absorbed by the advancing Burman. Pyū cities were eventually abandoned by their inhabitants following the fall of Halingyi. The last mention of the Pyū can be found at Bagan in the Rajakumar inscription of 1113 CE. After that the Pyū and Pyū script disappear from history.

ARAKAN

There is no archaeological evidence to support who the earliest inhabitants of Arakan were. Most likely they included some of the ethnic groups that live in the more remote areas of the present-day Rakhine state of the Union of Myanmar: the Chin, the Kami, the Mro, and the Sak. The first evidence of the Arakanese themselves dates from the ninth century CE. This suggests that the Arakanese were originally one of the Pyū tribes that crossed the Arakan Yomo following the destruction of the Pyū polities by the armies of the Nan-Chou. The early polities were located in the valleys and floodplains of the Kaladan and Lemro Rivers.

The Arakanese chronicles date the origins of the Arakan people to 3000 BCE and the legendary founder of Dhanyawadi, Marayu. The chronicles further state that a series of 60 kings from the four cities of Lemro River valley ruled Arakan until 1404 CE. It is only in the fourth century BCE that other sources contribute to the history of Arakan. Given that the sources or inscriptions that were excavated were written in Sanskrit, suggest that the origins of Arakan's founders were Indian, rather than Tibeto-Burman. The historical record of

Arakan begins with Ananda Candra inscription (ca. 729 CE) that describes the founding of the Candra dynasty by King Dvancandra (r. ca. 370–425 CE) found in the city that has come to be known today as Dhanyawadi. Dhanyawadi, the capital of the first Arakanese kingdom is a corruption of the Pali word Dhannavati, meaning "blessed with grain." Dhanyawadi was the center of a vast trade network that extended between China in the east and Persia and India to the west.

As power shifted from Dhanyawadi in the sixth century CE, the second Arakanese kingdom to emerge was Vesali (Wethali). The city of Vesali was founded in 788 CE by Maha Taing Candra who reigned for a period of 22 years. Situated northeast of the Sittwe River, Vesali lies 44 miles inland from the Bay of Bengal on the Ram Chaung, a tributary of the Kaladan River. Over time, the city became an important trading port. Using the wealth obtained from trade Candra kings extended their territory as far north as Chittagong. According to the Ananda Candra pillar inscription at least 22 kings reigned during the Vesali dynasty that was characterized by peace and prosperity. Archaeological and numismatic evidence indicate that Vesali's wealth was based on trade between pre-Bagan Myanmar, China and the Mons, and India, Bengal, and Persia. Buddhism thrived in Vesali as evidenced by the number of pagodas, stupas, monasteries, and shrines found throughout Vesali. Records from the Buddhist Synod convened in 638 CE indicate the presence of 1,000 Buddhist monks from Vesali. Vesali began to decline in the 10th century CE following large-scale migration of the Burman from the eastern Himalayas of the Tibetan Plateau. The dynasty came to an abrupt end in 957 CE when the Mongols killed Sula Taing Candra, the last king of the Candra dynasty. According to the Arakanese chronicles Sula Taing Candra was succeeded by Mraw Chaung Amarathu, a Mro chieftain who married Candra Devi, the widow of Sula Taing Candra. Amarathu was succeeded by his nephew Paipru. Toward the end of the 10th century, the Pyū invaded Vesali.

THE CITIES OF THE LEMRO VALLEY (11TH TO THE 15TH CENTURIES)

From the 11th to the 15th centuries a series of small Arakanese cities emerged along the lowlands west of the Lemro River, as the alluvial flood plains of the valley proved ideal for cultivation. Little is known about the early history of the cities of the Lemro valley. It is thought that the earliest indigenous inhabitants were the Chin, Kami, Mro, and Sak tribes. The Arakanese (Rakhine) are thought to be of Tibeto-Burman origin, who began crossing the Arakan Yoma Range in the ninth century. The Arakanese eventually displaced the indigenous tribes of the Lemro valley. The Arakanese went on to found a series of settlements at Sambawak (794–818), Pyinsa (818–1103), Parein (1103–1123), Hkrit (1142–1154), second Sambawak (1154–1163), Myohaung Toungoo (1163–1251), and Launggret (1247–1433), along the banks of the Lemro River. These royal capitals had both cultural and political links to Bagan. Capitals changed as succeeding dynasties moved locations to suit either political or military objectives.

The oldest city, Sambawak, is believed to have been built by Saw Shwe Lu (r. ca. 794–818), a descendent of the Candra kings of Vesali on the west bank of the Lemro River in 794. Invasions of Tibeto-Burman tribes from the east and the revolt of the native Sak tribe destabilized the kingdom. Unable to defend itself from neighboring Bagan's military might, Sambawak eventually became a part of Bagan. According to different Arakanese chronicles, Pyinsa was founded by Nga Ton Min (r. ca. 818–828). Twelve kings ruled the city for over 250 years during a period of relative calm and stability. It was during a period of political turmoil during the reign of Min Bilu (r. ca. 1075–1078) that a noble named Thinkhaya (r. ca. 1078–1092) assassinated Min Bilu, usurping the crown and forcing the royal family to seek refuge at the court of the king of Bagan, Kyanzittha. The royal family would remain in exile for 25 years before returning to Pyinsa. According to legend, Kyanzittha sent an army of 100,000 Pyūs and 100,000 Tailangs to restore Min Bula's grandson, Letyaminnan (r. ca. 1103–1109) to the throne. Once restored to the throne, Letyaminnan moved the capital to Parein in 1103. Parein's day as the capital would come to an end when the last king of the Parein dynasty, Min Phu Sa, moved the capital to Hkrit in an effort to make the capital easier to defend.

Hkrit was occupied only for 12 years as ecological problems forced Danuyupol (r. ca. 1151–1160) to abandon the newly built city. Sambawak was reoccupied in 1154, beginning the short-lived second Sambawak dynasty. Danuyupol was assassinated by a noble named Salangarbo (r. ca. 1160–1161) in 1160. Salangarbo was in turn replaced by Myitzuthin (r. ca. 1161–1163) who moved the capital to Myohaung Toungoo to the east bank of the Lemro River. Seventeen kings ruled for Myohaung Toungoo for a period of 85 years before the last king of the dynasty, Alawmarphyun moved the capital to Launggret. Launggret was founded by the legendary King Mun Htee in 1247, at a time when Bagan's power was beginning to wane. According the Arakanese chronicles Mun Htee ruled for 96 years. Under Mun Htee Launggret managed to become independent and began to expand its authority west into Bengal, Cape Negrais in the south, and to the west bank of the Ayeyarwaddy in the east. Following the founding of Launggret, the Arakanese chronicles detail a turbulent 12th century CE. This period saw a Talaing invasion in the south, a weakening of the legitimacy of the monarch, and several usurpers to the throne.

The Lemro period would come to an end in 1406 when Burmese forces led by Min Khaung Yaza occupied Launggret and deposed Min Saw Mon who fled to the court of Gaisuddin Azam Shah in Gaur, the capital of the Bengal sultanate. Min Saw Mon as Suleiman Shah (r. ca. 1430–1433) stayed in exile in Gaur for 24 years before regaining his throne in 1430 and built the new capital city of Mrauk-U. Min Saw Mon's Bengali followers were allowed to settle in and around Mrauk-U, thus becoming the earliest Muslim settlers in Arakan. Muslim rule and influence in Arakan lasted for more than 350 years.

THE MRAUK-U DYNASTY (1430–1784)

According to the Arakanese chronicles Min Saw Mon as Suleiman Shah is considered the founder of the Mrauk-U dynasty. Min Saw Mon and his successors adopted the custom of taking a Muslim name. It is said that he was exiled from Arakan by invading Burmese troops from the kingdom of Ava. After 24 years in exile Min Saw Mon regained control of the throne with military support of Gaisuddin Azam Shah, the sultan of Bengal. In return for the sultan's assistance the Suleiman Shah agreed to cede southern Chittagong to Bengal and pay an annual tribute. According to the Arakanese chronicles, Mrauk-U would remain a part of Bengal sultans for about 100 years. It is of note that no further sources can confirm the Mrauk-U founding myth. Subsequent Arakanese kings extended their control over the Arakanese littoral to the coastal areas and the islands of Cheduba and Ramree through a combination of force and diplomacy.

Min Saw Mon was succeeded by his brother Min Kahri Ali Khan (r. ca. 1434–1459), who brought the Arakanese littoral under Mrauk-U suzerainty. Ali Khan campaigned against Chittagong, Cukkara, and Ramu during his reign. He entered into a friendship and border treaty with King Naripati of Ava and declared Arakan free from Bengali rule. Ali Khan's son and successor Ba Saw Phru Kalima Shah (r. ca. 1459–1482) defeated Sultan Barbak Shaw of Bengal and occupied Chittagong in 1459. Kalima Shah was assassinated in 1482 and Mrauk-U was plunged into chaos for a short period of time before Dawlya Mathu Shah (r. ca. 1482–1492) ascended the throne. Dawlya Mathu Shah extended Mrauk-U's control to the east and west. Little is known about the 50-year period following the reign of Dawlya Mathu Shah. What is known is that a series of succession struggles weakened Mrauk-U kingdom to the extent that they lost control over the Arakanese littoral until the reign of Min Bin Zabuk Shah (r. ca. 1531–1553).

Min Bin's reign is considered to be most important in Arakanese history as it was during his reign that Arakan defeated Burmese king Tabinshweti's invasion, aided by Portuguese mercenaries and Mon levies, in 1546–1547. Min Bin took advantage of the Mughals' invasion of the sultanate of Gaur to occupy east Bengal with a combined fleet and army movement that ended with the capture of Chittagong. Min Bin is also credited with creating a naval fleet that dominated the Bay of Bengal and the Gulf of Martaban. This allowed the Mrauk-U dynasty to control the entire coast line of the Dacca and the Sundarbans to Yankon and Moulmein, a distance of 1,000 miles. Ports along the coast received Arab, Danish, Dutch, and Portuguese traders during this period. Controlling the economies of the Kaladan and Lemro valleys led to growing international trade that enabled Mrauk-U to become prosperous.

The reigns of Min Phalaung Sikendar Shah (r. ca. 1571–1593), his son Min Rajagri Salim Shah I (r. ca. 1593–1612), and his grandson Min Khamuang Hussain Shah (r. ca. 1612–1622) strengthened the wealth and power of Mrauk-U kingdom. In 1580, Min Phalaung defeated the Burmese king Bayinnaung's attempt to invade Arakan. In 1598, Min Rajagri temporarily allied himself with the king of Toungoo and conquered the Mon capital of Pegu. Taking advantage of the power vacuum in Lower Burma, he then attacked and occupied the port city of Syriam. Once in control of Syriam, he appointed Portuguese mercenary and adventurer Philip de Brito e Nicota to administer the newly acquired territory. De Brito, however, had other plans. He expelled the Arakanese governor and held Syriam under the authority of the Viceroy of Goa, a Portuguese colony since the 15th century. In 1604, he defeated an attempt by Min Rajagri to attack Syriam. De Brito then forged an alliance with the Mon king Binnya Dala though marriage. In 1612, de Brito e Nicota and the king of Martaban launched an invasion of Toungoo. The king of Toungoo responded by sending forces to Syriam. The city would eventually fall in 1613 when a Mon chief opened the city's gates to let Anaukhpetlun's forces in. Following a period of turmoil in Bengal, Min Khamuang seized control of Chittagong.

Min Khamuang was succeeded by his son Thri Thudhamma Salim Shah II (r. ca. 1622–1638). His reign was characterized by a period of relative prosperity as foreign trade brought wealth. Thri Thudhamma was poisoned by Queen Nat Shin Mai. Following his death, his son Min Sanay became king. He ruled for only 21 days before he, too, was poisoned by Queen Nat Shan Mai. The queen's consort minister Nga Kutha was declared king with the title Narapaigyi (r. ca. 1638–1645). He then went on to a large number of royal clansmen and ministers to consolidate control. Narapaigyi was succeeded by his son Thadu Mintra (r. ca. 1645–1652) who was succeeded by his son Sanda Thudhamma (r. ca. 1652–1684). The death of Sanda Thudhamma brought a period of political instability to Arakan. A century of chaos followed in which the political authority broke down as a series of kings occupied the throne. From 1685 to 1710 there were 10 kings who reigned for an average of two and a half years. By the middle of the 17th century political order had completely broke down.

The Mrauk-U dynasty would continue until the late 18th century, when a power struggle among the Arakanese nobility was exploited by the Burmans. In 1782, Thadoe Aung, the duke of Rambree, ascended the throne. He was accorded the regal sounding title of "Mahasamada" (great elect president) by the Mun Ataiban (the royal assembly of lords). A rival noble, Ngathande, the duke of Ngasaraingchaung, sent a request to King Bodawpaya to invade Arakan and overthrow Thadoe Aung. In December 1784, a 30,000-strong Burmese force invaded Mrauk-U. Arakanese forces were caught off-guard and suffered a crushing defeat. The capital was left in ruins as mosques, temples, shrines, seminaries, and libraries were put to the torch. Thadoe Aung was forced into exile; his court, the Brahmins, as well as many Arakanese artisans and nobility were taken to Upper Burma, while over 200,000 refugees fled to the jungles of Chittagong.

3

Bagan (1044–1287) and Small Kingdoms (1287–1531)

HISTORICAL AND CULTURAL BACKGROUND

There is some dispute as to the origins of the first Burmese empire at Bagan. Early research did not address the question of the origins of Bagan but focused on understanding Bagan's history, culture, and society. It wasn't until the issue of ethnicity and language appeared in Burmese history textbooks did the issue of the first inhabitants of Bagan become salient. Establishing the origins of Bagan has been hampered by lack of source material (e.g., inscriptions and/or epigraphs) from the Bagan period. Unfortunately, under King Bodawpaya many of the inscriptions were removed and taken to Amarapuvo in the late 18th century. Tradition established by local chronicles suggests Bagan was founded by the Pyū king Thamoddarit in the first century CE and that the original inhabitants were Pyū, although this claim cannot be substantiated. The Glass Palace Chronicle indicates that Bagan, formerly known as Arimaddanapura (the city of the enemy crusher) and also as Tambadipa (the land of copper) or Tassadessa (the parched land), was founded in 849 during the reign of Pyinbya (r. ca. 846–878). Lacking either definitive archaeological or epigraphical evidence, there can only be speculation regarding the origins of Bagan, neither of which is grounded in fact nor without its detractors.

It wasn't until Arawrahtā (r. ca. 1044–1077) ascended the throne in the mid-11th century CE that Bagan began to dominate Upper Burma. As king, Arawrahtā invaded and defeated the Mon kingdom in 1057. He captured the Mon capital of Thaton and carried off 30,000 Mon captives back to Bagan, unifying Burma for the first time. The defeat of the Mon proved to be an important event in the cultural history of Bagan as many of the Mon captives were Therāvāda Buddhist monks who converted the Burman to Buddhism.

Following the defeat of the Mon, Arawrahtā sent monks to Ceylon to bring back original texts, receiving teachers at his court, as well as embarking on an ambitious temple-building program at Bagan using Mon craftsmen and architects as well as the conquered wealth of Thaton to support the sangha. Religious scholarship flourished to the extent that monks from Ceylon began traveling to Bagan to study. Arawrahtā's successors Kyanzittha (r. ca. 1084–1112) and Alaugsithu (r. ca. 1112–1167) consolidated control over what is modern-day Myanmar and oversaw the construction of more than 2,000 temples and pagodas as well as thousands of stupas in a 25-square-mile area around Bagan. Radiocarbon dating of inscriptions found on Buddhist shrines and temples in Bagan indicate that they were built sometime between the 11th and 13th centuries CE.

Bagan would reach its cultural and artistic zenith during the early to mid-12th century. Following the reign of Alaugsithu, Bagan's power slowly waned. The kingdom at Bagan would continue to rule Burma until 1287, when it was invaded by the Mongol army following King Narathihapati's refusal to pay tribute to Kublai Khan. Even though the Mongols installed Narathihapati's son Kyawswa as a puppet ruler, the kingdom of Bagan quickly disintegrated into rival kingdoms as Arakan, Pegu, and the Mon city-states of the Moncon valley rose in rebellion against Bagan.

Following the sacking of Bagan, Lower Burma fragmented into a number of smaller city-states. Semi-autonomous kingdoms emerged at Bassein-Myaungma, Pegu, and Martaban. The Mon withdrew to the south, where they regained their independence, capturing Martaban and Pegu and reestablishing their old kingdom, Hanthawaddy Pegu (1287–1580), and controlling much of Lower Burma. In Upper Burma a series of small Shan kingdoms, Myinsaing, Pinya, and Sagaing, dominated the Ayeyarwaddy and expanded into what is now the Kachin state and along the Chindwin River. The Shan chieftain Wareru (r. ca. 1287–1306) used the power vacuum to form an alliance with Tarabya, the ambitious Mon governor of Pegu and the two of them jointly seized control of Pegu and ousted the Burmese governor, occupying much of the area south of Pyi and Toungoo. Once he was in control of Lower Burma Wareru had Tarabya executed. Wareru declared himself king, shifted his capital from Madana to Pegu, and founded the Ava dynasty near modern Mandalay at the meeting of the Ayeyarwaddy and Myitnge Rivers. It wasn't until the reign of Thadominpaya (r. ca. 1364–1368) that Ava controlled Upper Burma and to which the kingdom is dated. Ava used their geographical location on the eastern bank of the Ayeyarwaddy to exploit Chinese overland trade as well as Indian Ocean commerce. Following the Mongol destruction of the kingdom of Dali in the late 13th century, a migration of ethnic Shan tribes from the mountains of southern Yunnan into the Nam Mao valley and surrounding region filled the void left by the fall of the Bagan kingdom. The period following the collapse of the kingdom of Bagan was characterized by constant warfare between Ava and Pegu, and to a lesser extent between Ava and the Shan principalities as Ava sought to reassert suzerainty over Burma. Ava briefly controlled Arakan (1379–1420) and came close to defeating Pegu, but could never unify Burma again.

THE ORIGINS OF BAGAN

To this day the origins of Bagan remain unclear. Local chronicles suggests that a line of 55 kings ruled over Bagan for a period of 12 centuries. The chronicles go on to claim that Bagan was originally one of the group of 19 villages practicing wet-rice agriculture, and existing as a contemporary to the Pyū city-states of Beikthano, Halingyi, and Śrī Kṣetra circa 107 CE. The difficulty with affixing a date this early in Burmese history is that it is not supported by either archaeological or epigraphical evidence.

Archaeological evidence as well as Bagan's location between Halingyi in the north and Śrī Kṣetra in the south point suggest that Bagan had Pyū origins. The Burmans began migrating from Nan-Chou in present-day Yunnan to the Ayeyarwaddy valley in the sixth century. Over time the Burman established themselves at Bagan, gradually displacing the Pyū. When the Nan-Chou kingdom invaded and sacked Halingyi in ca. 832–835, it destroyed the last major Pyū center in Upper Burma, thereby creating a power vacuum into which the Burmans stepped, displacing Pyū influence. The local chronicles go on to state that it was Pyinbya (r. ca. 846–878) who built the present-day Bagan city wall in 849 CE following the transfer of the capital from Tampawady. By 874 CE, Bagan had become a major city and by the 11th century it was a burgeoning regional power in Southeast Asia.

THE RISE AND FALL OF BAGAN

The ascension of Arawrahtā marked the rise of Bagan as a regional power in Southeast Asia. Prior to the 11th century there were two rival centers of power in Burma, the Mon kingdom at Thaton and Bagan. Following the conquest of Thaton, Arawrahtā marched to Śrī Kṣetra, expanding Bagan's influence and asserting hegemony over what is present-day Burma. He consolidated control by drawing neighboring city-states into a vassal status arrangement and creating the first centralized government in Burma. Between 1057 and 1059, Arawrahtā led an army to Nan-Chou in search of the Buddha's tooth relic. As he returned to Bagan the Shan kingdom of Mong Mao Long swore allegiance to Arawrahtā. Arawrahtā's successors Kyanzittha (r. ca. 1084–1112) and Alaugsithū (r. ca. 1112–1167) consolidated control over Burma.

Arawrahtā transformed Bagan into the religious and cultural center of Southeast Asia. He made Therāvāda Buddhism the state religion and received the complete Tripitaka, the earliest collection of Buddhist writings, from Ceylon. As a consequence of the religious scholarship, Buddhist monks and students from Yunnan, Laos, Thailand, and India came to study at Bagan. By the early 12th century Bagan had become a cosmopolitan center of Buddhist studies. It was during this period that many of the temples, pagodas, and stupas were built. Kyanzittha and his successors built more than 2,000 pagodas as well as thousands of lesser shrines in the 25-mile radius around Bagan. He is known to have personally commissioned the famous Ananda pagoda in which there were over 500 images of the Buddha, as well as building a large number of temples and religious monuments. Many more large temples were built later during Alaugsithū's reign. Most notably, the Thatbyinnya temple, Shwegugyi temple (great golden cave), and Dhammayangyi temple were constructed.

Kyaswa's (r. ca. 1234–1250) ascension to the throne in 1234 marked the beginning of a period of decline of Bagan. His large-scale construction projects depleted the royal treasury. Weakened by the continued expansion of tax-free religious landholdings and estates, the authority of the state weakened. Buddhism began to undermine the legitimacy of the state as religious endowments increased, while tax revenues decreased. Unable to reform the monastic establishment Kyaswa chose to withdraw from public life, preferring to compose religious writings, while leaving the administration of his kingdom to his son Uzana (r. ca. 1250–1254). The power behind the throne during Kyaswa's reign, Uzana was killed by an elephant in a hunting accident in Dala shortly into his reign. Following Uzana's untimely death, his youngest son Narathihapati (r. ca. 1254–1287) was placed on the throne by the ambitious chief court minister Yazathingyan, who believed he could control the young prince. Once Narathihapati assumed the throne he promptly exiled Yazathingyan. Narathihapati would be the last ruler of Bagan, ending the nearly 250-year rule of Bagan over the Ayeyarwaddy River basin.

THE MONGOL INVASIONS

Following the subjugation of the Dali kingdom of Yunnan (937–1253) in 1253, Kublai Khan sent an envoy to Burma to demand tribute and allegiance from the Burmese king. According to some sources, Narathihapati refused to meet the first of the emissaries. Two years later Kublai Khan sent three more envoys to demand tribute. This time Narathihapati executed the envoys and sent their heads back to Kublai Khan. Confident of victory and emboldened by the lack of response from Kublai Khan, Narathihapati invaded the neighboring state of Kaungai in 1277. Despite being heavily outnumbered by the Burmese who were led by scores of war elephants, local garrisons of Mongol troops were able to decisively defeat the Burmese at the battle of Ngasaunggyan. Kublai Khan then sent Nasir al-Din, the son of his trusted retainer Saiyid Ajall, into Burma with the objective of taking Bagan. The Mongols continued their southward advance into Burma until heat and exhaustion forced them to return to China.

Marco Polo arrived in Burma as the official envoy of Kublai Khan in 1278, a year after the Mongols defeated the Burmese at the battle of Ngasaunggyan. He describes a battle that took place the previous year in the Vochan valley between the Mongol cavalry and a much larger Burmese army. Despite having over 2,000 war elephants and a combination of 60,000 horsemen and light infantrymen, a force of 12,000 well-equipped Mongol cavalrymen was able to defeat the Burmese. Unable to confront the Burmese war elephants head on, the Mongol cavalry dismounted and launched volley after volley of arrows at the elephants. Frightened by the shower of arrows the elephants panicked, turned around, and ran away. In the confusion, the Mongol cavalry remounted their horses and charged after the Burmese.

Led by Prince Sangudar, the Mongols again invaded Burma in 1283. The Mongols attacked the border fortresses at Htigyaing and Tagaung near Bhamo and quickly defeated the Burmese army, opening the Ayeyarwaddy River valley to invasion. Frightened by the prospect of being taken captive by the Mongols, Narathihapati fled southward to Bassein and offered submission to the Mongol Empire, thus earning the nickname Tarokpyemin (the king who ran away from the Chinese). Having lost the respect of his people following his cowardly retreat following the battle of Bhamo, Narathihapati was assassinated by his second son Thihathu as he tried to return to Bagan. Thihathu then fought his two brothers who were rivals to the throne. Taking advantage of the political turmoil created following the assassination of Narathihapati, Kublai Khan's grandson Temür led a large Mongol army down the Ayeyarwaddy River valley, captured Bagan, and deposed Thihathu. After taking Bagan the Mongols went on to sack the city, destroying thousands of pagodas, temples, and stupas. In the aftermath of the sacking of Bagan the Tai Shan briefly gained control over the Ayeyarwaddy valley, the Shan plateau, Laos, Thailand, and Assam, only to be forced from northern Burma the following decade when the Mongols installed Narathihapati's son Kyawswa (r. ca. 1287–1298), who then submitted to Mongol vassalage. The Mongols incorporated northern Burma into their empire as the province of Chêng-mien but internal power struggles weakened Bagan as various court factions jockeyed for power.

Responding to a request from Prince Tribhuvanaditya, Temür dispatched a detachment of the Mongol army to Burma in 1297. The Mongols were able to successfully expel the Shans from northern Burma. In 1299, the Shans again invaded Bagan and killed Prince Tribhuvanaditya, the last member of the Burmese royal family. The following year Temür launched a punitive raid into Burma in reprisal for the assassination of Prince Tribhuvanaditya. The expedition ended when a Mongol commander accepted a bribe from the Shans and returned to China. After that, the Mongols lost interest in Burma, never to return. Burma then entered a phase of political disintegration and cultural decay for the next three centuries until the emergence of the Toungoo dynasty.

HANTHAWADDY PEGU (1287–1540)

Following the fall of Bagan in 1287, the Mon withdrew to the south and reestablished their old kingdom in Lower Burma. Under Wareru, the son-in-law of Rāma Gāmhèn of Sukhothai, the Mon captured the cities of Martaban and Pegu, thus establishing Mon control over Lower Burma. As Pegu began to dominate Lower Burma, the capital was shifted to Pegu in 1369. Pegu would prosper under the Wareru dynasty and remain the capital of the Mon kingdom of Ramanadesa from 1369 to 1539, when it fell to the Burman.

Pegu's rise to prominence is associated with the reign of Rajadhirit (r. ca. 1385–1423) as he launched a series of military campaigns against the Ava kings Mingyiswasawke (r. ca. 1368–1401) and his son, Minkhaung (r. ca. 1401–1422). Rajadhirit's death in 1423 set off a succession struggle as a number of royal claimants emerged. Rajadhirit was finally succeeded by his daughter, Queen Shinsawbu (r. ca. 1453–1492) in 1453. During the interregnum Pegu began to prosper as a commercial and trading center, exporting rice to both India and Malaysia. Pegu also took advantage of the increase in maritime trade in the Indian Ocean to extend its control of the port cities of Bassein-Myaungma, Dala-Syriam, and Sandoway. It was during this period of commercial expansion that Europeans first came to Burma. In 1435, a Venetian trader named Nicolo di Conti became the first European to visit Burma. He stayed in Pegu for four months and described what he saw in his diaries. Other European merchants would follow in di Conti's footsteps. In 1496, during the reign of Binnya Ran (r. ca. 1492–1526), a Russian merchant named Nikitin and a Genoese merchant, Hieronymo Santo Stefano, also visited Pegu.

Queen Shinsawbu was succeeded by the former Buddhist monk Dhammazedi (r. ca. 1472–1492). The reign of Dhammazedi is considered to be Pegu's golden age, as he oversaw the purification of Buddhism in Pegu. Upon his ascension to the throne Dhammazedi found confusion and doctrinal differences over Buddhist practices. Buddhism was, in his view as a former Buddhist monk, deteriorating. The sangha was divided into sects over the interpretation of monastic rules. Monasteries and monks were conducting ecclesiastical acts separately. Dhammazedi was convinced the only way sasana could be unified and purified was the restoration of higher ordination. As such, he sent 22 monks and 33 novices to Ceylon to undergo re-ordination according to the Singhalese tradition. In fact the northern Tai and Burmese chronicles as well as the Kālyaṇī inscriptions document several religious missions to Ceylon from Ava and Pegu. In return, Sīnala monks visited Pegu.

In 1530, the then 16-year-old Tabengshweti (r. ca. 1531–1550) of the Toungoo kingdom decided to reunite Burma. Tabengshweti captured the port city of Bassein in 1535 and went on to attack Pegu. He attacked the city three times, eventually capturing Pegu in 1539. Tabengshweti celebrated his victory over Pegu by decorating the Shwedagon pagoda and other pagodas with plundered gold.

THE HEIR TO BAGAN: THE RISE
AND FALL OF AVA (1364–1555)

The Burman kingdom of Ava (1364–1555), the successor state to the Myinsaing (1298–1312), Pinya (1312–1364), and Sagaing (1315–1364) kingdoms, emerged about a century after the fall of Bagan. Ava was founded on January 26, 1365, by a young Burmese nobleman named Thadominpaya (r. ca. 1364–1368) who seized control of an area at the confluence of the Ayeyarwaddy and Myitnge Rivers. Thadominpaya sought to unite the Burman, Mon, and Shans into a single nation as they were under the kings of Bagan. He began by gradually consolidating control over Upper Burma. He led a series of military campaigns to subjugate the cities of Taungdwingyi and Segu between 1365 and 1367. Thadominpaya died during his military campaign to Segu and was succeeded by his brother-in-law Mingyiswasawke (r. ca. 1368–1401). During his long reign, Mingyiswasawke consolidated regional power at Ava by conquering Kyaukse, Meikhtila, Minbu, the Mu valley, and Yamthin. These areas not only provided Ava with a stable source of food but also gave Ava additional manpower reserves. This additional manpower provided Ava with the military strength necessary to wage continuous wars against her neighbors. During the reigns of Mingaung (r. ca. 1401–1422), Thihathu (r. ca. 1422–1425), and Naripati (r. ca. 1442–1468), Ava reached its zenith. Domestic political stability gave the Ava kings the opportunity to wage continued warfare against Hanthawaddy Pegu, Arakan, and the Shan mongs (city-states) in an attempt to reassert suzerainty over Burma. Ava briefly controlled Arakan (1379–1420) and came close to defeating Pegu, but could never unify Burma again. By the 1480s the continuous wars waged against Hanthawaddy Pegu and the Shan states created political instability in Ava. The power of Ava began to wane between 1480 and 1520 as internal strife weakened the state. The Mong Yang ruler Shwenankyawshin launched a series of raids against Ava and its allies between 1524 and 1527. Eventually the Shan principality of Mong Yang launched a series of raids that culminated in the capture of Ava in 1527. A Mong Yang–led confederation of Shan mongs ruled Upper Burma until the Shan mongs began to disintegrate. When King Tabengshweti's son-in-law Bayinnaung (r. ca. 1554–1584) ascended the throne, he sought to reassert Burman control over Upper Burma, capturing Ava in 1555, and laying the foundations of the second Burmese empire, Toungoo.

4

The Toungoo (1531–1599) and Restored Toungoo Dynasties (1599–1752)

MIN-GYI-NYO, TABINSHWETI, AND THE FOUNDING OF THE TOUNGOO DYNASTY

The origins of the Toungoo dynasty lie in the downfall of the Ava dynasty. Toungoo emerged toward the end of the Ava dynasty when Burman refugees migrated southward to the Sittang valley following successive invasions of the Mong Yang Shan during the 1480s. The Burmese chronicles also recorded the Mong Yang Shan's conquest of Ava. During 1501–1502, Yamethin elites migrated south to Toungoo following a purge of the royal court after the assassination of the ruler of Yamethin.

King Min-gyi-nyo seized the throne of Toungoo in 1486 after murdering his uncle King Si-thu-nge. He then married the daughter of the king of Ava and was given Toungoo to rule. During the early 1490s, Min-gyi-nyo built a new capital and established himself as a military commander. After the Mon king Dhammazedi died in 1492, Min-gyi-nyo attacked settlements along the frontier between Ava and Toungoo. A year later, he attacked Kyaung-pya on the Toungoo-Ramanya frontier. During 1503–1504, Min-gyi-nyo made the decision to depopulate the settlements he was given by the king of Ava.

Sometime between 1505 and 1506, Min-gyi-nyo forged an alliance with the cities of Prome and Taungdwingi. For the next five years, he waged a series of campaigns around the region near Bagan. In 1510, King Min-gyi-nyo founded the first Toungoo dynasty at Toungoo. It was Min-gyi-nyo's son and heir King Tabinshweti (r. ca. 1531–1556) who consolidated control over both Upper and Lower Burma, uniting most of Burma when he captured the port city of Bassein and defeated the Mon capital of Pegu. Sixteen-year-old Tabinshweti succeeded his father as ruler in 1531. Not content with ruling Upper Burma, Tabinshweti planned on expanding Toungoo by invading Pegu. Controlling Pegu would give Toungoo access to its abundant natural wealth and direct access to the international maritime trade and foreign mercenaries. He captured the Mon port city of Bassein in the Ayeyarwaddy delta in 1535. Pegu finally fell in 1539 when Tabinshweti occupied the city and forced the Mon king Tushintakayutpi (r. ca. 1526–1538) to flee to Prome. He then transferred the capital from Toungoo to Pegu and was recognized as the undisputed king of Lower Burma. Tabinshweti then held a double coronation ceremony in both Pegu and Bagan to demonstrate that he ruled both Upper and Lower Burma. He built his palace on the site of the old Mon city. Following the unification of Burma in 1539, Tabinshweti attempted two unsuccessful campaigns against Tavoy and Ayutthaya, the Siamese capital in 1548, only to be forced to return to Pegu. Humiliated by the crushing defeats Tabinshweti retreated from public life before being assassinated by a close Mon advisor Smim Sawhtut in 1551. Smim Sawhtut crowned himself king but was in turn killed by Smim Htaw, the son of the last king of Pegu, who led a Mon army to Pegu, where Smim Sawhtut was executed after ruling for only three months.

Tabinshweti's brother-in-law and eventual successor King Bayinnaung (r. ca. 1551–1581) crushed the Mon revolt in Toungoo, killed Smim Htaw, and installed himself as king. He then led his army south, capturing the city of Pegu and executing Smim Htaw, the son of the last Mon king of Pegu. Under Bayinnaung's rule, the port of Pegu would come to dominate the maritime trade of mainland Southeast Asia. Following the consolidation of control of both Upper Burma and Lower Burma, Bayinnaung set about expanding his empire. Bayinnaung launched a series of military campaigns from Upper Burma that culminated in Toungoo's control of Ayutthaya, Lon Chang, and the Shan states. In 1555, he defeated the Shan at Ava, placing them under Burmese suzerainty for the first time. Between 1555 and 1557, Bayinnaung led two additional campaigns in which he conquered the Shan states to the north and east. Alarmed by Bayinnaung's victory over the Shans, the Tai of Chiang Mai formulated rebellion among the Shan Sawbwas. Bayinnaung's response to the Tai interference was swift. He crossed the Salween River and conquered Chiang Mai in 1558. Bayinnaung's defeat of Chiang Mai served as a signal to the Shan chieftains on the China-Toungoo border to swear allegiance to Bayinnaung.

Following the defeat of Chiang Mai, Bayinnaung became involved in a Tai power struggle. Settatirat, the king of Laos, invaded Chiang Mai in 1558. The following year Settatirat forged an alliance with Toungoo's historical enemy, Siam, and moved his capital to the fortified city of Ayutthaya. Settatirat attacked the Siamese capital of Ayutthaya in 1563. For a short period of time, Toungoo was the most powerful state in Southeast Asia. Bayinnaung invaded Siam again in 1568 in response to the attack on Pitsanulok by the former king of Siam. Initially repulsed by the lethal firepower of Portuguese mercenaries employed by the Siamese, Bayinnaung laid siege to Pitsanulok. Unable to break the stalemate, Bayinnaung used the former Ayutthaya minister Paya Charki to trick the city's defenders into weakening their defenses. Bayinnaung took the city, executed the sub-king, and replaced him with the governor of Pitsanulok, Mahadhammaraja Dipiti. Bayinnaung then marched to Laos but failed to capture Settatirat.

Legal scholarship flourished during Bayinnaung's reign. A commission of 12 monks produced a compendium of Burmese legal writings. Other noted jurists compiled commentaries of Burmese customary law. Bayinnaung himself passed a series of legal rulings, which were collected and published. Bayinnaung's aim was to unite the various tribes of Burma under a common system of law, a common literature, and a common system of weights and measurements.

Bayinnaung's death in 1581 signaled the beginning of the end of the Toungoo dynasty, as a war of succession led to the eventual disintegration of the empire Bayinnaung had put together. It gave Ayutthaya the opportunity to regain its independence and shortly thereafter other city-states followed.

THE FALL OF TOUNGOO AND THE EMERGENCE OF THE RESTORED TOUNGOO DYNASTY (1597–1752)

Bayinnaung's son and successor Nanda Bayin (r. ca. 1581–1599) was the last monarch of the Toungoo dynasty, who was forced to quell numerous rebellions during his tumultuous reign. Upon succession to the throne, Nanda Bayin was immediately faced with a rebellion by his uncle, the viceroy of Ava. Nanda Bayin was able to defeat his uncle but was unable to subjugate their allies, Ayutthaya. In 1595, faced with the prospect of widespread rebellion and the potential loss of sovereignty to Portuguese interests, the rulers of Toungoo withdrew from Lower Burma and founded a second dynasty, the Restored Toungoo dynasty at Ava, following the sacking of Pegu by a combination of Arakanese and mutinous Toungoo forces. A rebellion led by Prince Naresuan defeated several of Nanda Bayin's armies, while Nanda Bayin himself was killed during his fifth invasion of Siam.

Bayinnaung's son and Nanda Bayin's half brother Nyaunggan Min was one of the many claimants to the Burmese throne following the deposition of Nanda Bayin. Instead of contesting his claim to the throne with other claimants, Nyaunggan Min focused on recapturing the Shan states and deflecting the interest of neighboring Siam. This is why Nyaunggan Min is referred to as the founder of the Restored Toungoo or Nyaunggan dynasty at Ava. Throughout his brief reign (r. ca. 1599–1606), Nyaunggan Min managed to reestablish suzerainty over Upper Burma and the surrounding Shan states. His death in 1606 ushered in the reign of his son Anaukhpetlun (r. ca. 1605–1628). Anaukhpetlun began his reign by clearing the Ayeyarwaddy delta of Arakanese and their Mon and Portuguese allies by capturing the cities of Prome in 1607 and Toungoo in 1610. In 1612, Portuguese mercenary Philip de Brito y Nicote and the king of Martaban invaded Toungoo, plundered the city, and attacked the palace before the attack was halted. In response, King Anaukhpetlun sent land and river forces to Syriam, laying siege and blockading the city. Syriam would eventually fall in 1613 when a Mon chief opened the city's gates to let Anaukhpetlun's forces in. De Brito was executed and Anaukhpetlun consolidated his rule over the south. He then captured Martaban, Ye, and Tavoy, giving Toungoo control over the coastline from Bassein in the west to the Gulf of Martaban down the Tenasserim littoral to Tavoy.

The next year Anaukhpetlun and his brother, the future king Thalun (r. ca. 1629–1648), launched an invasion of Lan Na (Chiang Mai) to regain control of the Tai states east of the Salween River. Following his conquest of the Tai states, Anaukhpetlun then invaded neighboring Siam, occupying Tenasserim before being forced to withdraw by a combined force of Siamese and Portuguese troops. Having consolidated control over an area extending from Keng Tung in the east to Arakan in the west, from Tavoy in the south to Hsenwi in the north by 1626, Anaukhpetlun ordered the rebuilding of Pegu and turned it into the political and commercial capital of Lower Burma. He also resumed Indian Ocean maritime trade with neighboring states and kingdoms as well as European East India Companies.

Anaukhpetlun then set out to reform the royal bureaucracy in an effort to exercise direct rule over the entirety of Burma as opposed to just the capital of Ava. Between 1610 and the time of his death in 1628, Anaukhpetlun instituted a series of broad changes in the daily administration designed to curb the autonomy of provincial officials. In 1628, before Anaukhpetlun was able to finish reforming the bureaucracy, he was assassinated by his son Minyedaikpya, who had discovered his affair with one of his concubines, the daughter of Kengtung Sawbwa. Minyedaikpya was briefly installed as king by ministers at the court, while his uncles and contenders to the throne, Thalun and Minyekyawswa II, were on a military expedition in the Shan mongs. Nominally the king, Minyedaikpya never exerted control beyond the kingdom's capital of Pegu. Throughout 1628, his two uncles, Thalun and Minyekyawswa, who had marched back from Shan states, were in control of Upper Burma, while Lower Burma had revolted against his rule. In 1629, Thalun marched down from Ava to reconquer Pegu. In September of the same year, Minyedaikpyawas seized by the commander of palace guards and sent to Thalun, who promptly executed him.

In 1629, Thalun (r. ca. 1629–1648) ascended the throne. In 1635, he moved the capital to Ava and crowned himself king of Ava and made his brother Minye Kyawthwa the crown prince. Thalun was one of the most able of the monarchs of the Nyaunggan dynasty. He continued the wide-ranging administrative and financial reforms started by his brother, centralizing bureaucratic power in Ava, rather than in the provinces as it had previously been. Regional governors were now subservient to the king. He also undertook a landmark census between 1635 and 1638 that recorded the gentry's rights, population, and tax, as well as service obligations of the entire population of the Ayeyarwaddy River valley to get an accurate picture of the manpower available at his disposal. Following Thalun's death in 1648, the Nyaunggan dynasty experienced a slow and steady decline for the next 100 years. Instead of clarifying the issue of royal succession, administrative reforms diminished the power of the princes while strengthening the power of ministers. Burmese politics descended into princely-ministerial factions. A series of weak kings would continue to rule Burma until the mid-17th century until the overthrow of the last Toungoo monarch, Mahadhammaraja Dipiti (r. ca. 1733–1752).

By the mid-17th century, palace intrigues began undermining the authority of the king. Ministers and their patronage networks sought power and influence at the royal court. By the reign of Minye Kyawdin (r. ca. 1673–1698), the king no longer exercised any real political authority, as power had devolved and fragmented into the hands of ministers, with provincial officials allying themselves with one ministerial court faction or another in return for securing royal appointments. The usurpation of the crown diminished the state's authority. Taking advantage of weakened royal authority, provinces and vassal states slowly gained their independence from Ava. During the reign of King Tanin-ganwei (r. ca. 1714–1733), the kingdom of Lan Na (Chiang Mai) revolted and gained independence in 1725. In 1733, and again in 1735, armies from Manipuri led by Gharib Newaz invaded and plundered Burmese territory west of the Ayeyarwaddy.

The Mon revolts that began in 1740 challenged the power of the last monarch of Nyaunggan dynasty, eventually leading to its downfall. The Mon rebellion began in Pegu in 1740 when the Burman governor openly rebelled against the weak authority of Ava by proclaiming himself king of Pegu. Fed up with the continuing resource and taxation demands and unwilling to accept a Burmese king in Pegu, the Mon rebelled. Rioting ensued, and the pretender to the throne was murdered. The Ava king Mahadhammaraja Dipiti then installed his uncle as the new governor of Pegu. The installation of yet another Burman overlord triggered further rioting in Pegu in which the Mon went on to kill Burmese court officials. Mahadhammaraja Dipiti further exacerbated Mon-Burman tensions by ordering the massacre of the Mon in Pegu in retaliation for the killing of the court officials. The Gwe Shans used the conflict between the Mon and the Burmans to stage their own rebellion. With the aid and support of the Mon and Karen communities, the Shans were able to take Pegu in 1740. Following the conquest of Pegu, the Mon selected an ethnic Burman monk Smim Htaw Buddhaketi (r. ca. 1740–1747) to be the first king of the Restored kingdom of Pegu. Unable or unwilling to take charge of the government or to lead the army, Smim Htaw Buddhaketi left governing and command and control of the army to his prime minister, a Shan noble named Binnya Dala. Pegu launched invasions against its northern rivals Prome and Ava. Smim Htaw Buddhaketi abdicated the throne in 1747 and left for Chiang Mai. He was replaced by Binnya Dala (r. ca. 1747–1757), the last ruler of the Restored kingdom of Pegu.

In 1750, the Qing dynasty in China sent troops to support Mahadhammaraja Dipiti but were defeated by the Mons. After consolidating control over Lower Burma, Binnya Dala launched an invasion of Ava during the dry season of 1751–1752. The crown prince of Pegu (Binnya Dala's brother) led the Mon and Shan armies into the Upper Ayeyarwaddy and laid siege to the cities of Sagaing and Ava. Ava fell to the Mon in 1752, and Mahadhammaraja Dipiti, his court, and about 20,000 prisoners were captured and taken back to Pegu. Mahadhammaraja Dipiti remained in captivity for another two years before he was executed for his suspected involvement with his supporters in formulating a potential rebellion. Mahadhammaraja Dipiti's death ended the Restored Toungoo dynasty and heralded a short period of conflict between the Burman and the Mon before a Burman village chief in Ava, U Aung Zeiya, led a revolt against Mon rule. The Burmese attacked and defeated the Mon at Pegu in 1757, thus beginning the Konbaung dynasty (1752–1885).

5

The Konbaung Dynasty
(1752–1885)

THE RISE OF THE ALAÙNGPAYÀ AND THE
REUNIFICATION OF BURMA

The Konbaung dynasty succeeded the Restored Toungoo dynasty when King Alaùngpayà (r. ca. 1752–1760) was crowned king in the northern township of Shwebo in 1752. U Aung Zeiya of Moksobo (who is also known as Alaùngpayà) was a village chief when the Mon kingdom of Pegu invaded Ava in 1752. Utilizing his considerable leadership skills Alaùngpayà was able to rally other local village chiefs to defeat the invading Mon forces. Following successive victories against the Mon, Alaùngpayà was enthroned as king by his fellow village chiefs in 1752, thus founding the Konbaung dynasty (heaven's platform), the third and last Burman empire. The following year he recaptured Ava. In 1754, Alaùngpayà took advantage of the Burman revolt against the Mon at Prome to launch a military expedition against the Mon. In early 1755, the fall of Prome opened the way to the Ayeyarwaddy delta, where his army took a number of Mon cities. The following year he began a series of campaigns designed at uniting the Burmans. He captured Syriam, thus depriving Pegu of its source of foreign arms and reinforcements. In May 1757, he forced the capitulation of Pegu despite the fact that the Mon were aided by

French mercenaries. The mutinous Mon king Binnya Dala was captured and publicly executed during a religious festival at the Shwedagon pagoda in Rangoon. In the wake of the defeat to the Burman many Mon chose to emigrate to neighboring Ayutthaya rather than to assimilate. Following the capitulation of the Peguan court, Alaùngpayà sought to cut disassociate himself and his dynasty with the former Mon seat of power at Pegu by establishing a new chief port city in Lower Burma at the village of Dagon, which he renamed Rangoon.

Following his victory over the Mon, Alaùngpayà devoted himself to the administrative and military reorganization of Burma. As a former village headman, Alaùngpayà realized that the problems of court administration were linked to the emergence of ministerial cliques. In order to eliminate court rivalries among patrons at court he decreed that village headmen were to be directly tied to the royal court through a combination of formal institutional obligations and personal relationships. This was designed to promote a clearer line of succession. Alaùngpayà then reconstituted the manner in which military conscription was conducted. He changed the levies from fixed quotas to variables to allow provincial governors through local jurisdictions the flexibility to fill their assigned levy by circumstance. This accommodated demographic population shifts in much of southern and central Burma accompanying the collapse of the Restored Toungoo dynasty. At the same time Alaùngpayà reorganized the military; he also changed the method of taxation from in-kind taxes to cash taxes and from agricultural to commercial revenues.

In 1758, Alaùngpayà sought to pacify the Shan principalities between the Upper Ayeyarwaddy and Yunnan. He then turned his attention to securing control of Manipur and Siam, which had always been considered crucial for security of the Ayeyarwaddy basin. While Alaùngpayà was leading an expedition against Manipur, Mon rebels seized control of Rangoon, Syriam, and Dala. Local Burmese forces were able to defeat the Mon rebels before they fled to neighboring Ayutthaya, where they were sheltered by the Siamese court. Recognizing the fact that Burma's eastern frontier wouldn't be secure as long as an Ayutthaya-Mon alliance was in place, Alaùngpayà decided to attack the source of the Mon's support and sanctuary, the kingdom of Siam.

THE WAR WITH SIAM

Alaùngpayà and two of his sons, Naungdawgi and Hsinbyushin, would wage war on Siam for over 60 years. During the dry season of 1759, Alaùngpayà launched an invasion of Siam through Mergui and Tenasserim. King Borommaracha managed to confront Alaùngpayà outside the town of Kui with an army of 15,000 but was easily defeated. Subsequently, the Burmese went on to capture the cities of Phetburi, Ratburi, and Suphanburi on the Gulf of Siam on their way to lay siege to the Siamese capital of Ayutthaya in April

1760. The Burmese advanced to the outskirts of the city on April 11, 1760, but never laid siege to Ayutthaya. For reasons unknown, Alaùngpayà began a sudden retreat from Ayutthaya toward Martaban but died en route on May 11, 1760, in the village of Kinywa. Sources differ on the reasons for Alaùngpayà's retreat from Ayutthaya. Siamese sources suggest that Alaùng-payà was wounded by an exploding shell from a siege gun, while Burmese sources state that he died from dysentery. Whatever his malady, the condition was most likely the reason behind the sudden withdrawal.

Alaùngpayà's eldest son Naungdawgi (r. ca. 1760–1763) succeeded his fa-ther. Most of Naungdawgi brief reign was spent suppressing two major rebel-lions. His untimely death in 1763 allowed his younger brother Hsinbyushin (r. ca. 1763–1776) to ascend to the throne. Hsinbyushin, a seasoned military commander, launched a classic pincer movement against Ayutthaya in Sep-tember 1765. One force attacked Chiang Mai and Vientiane before invading the Chao Phraya River valley and then attacking Ayutthaya from the north. A second force attacked from the south. Ayutthaya finally fell on April 28, 1767, three years after the operation's inception. The victory was short-lived as the governor of Tak province of Siam, Taksin (r. ca. 1767–1782), soon expelled Hsinbyushin's armies from cities along the east coast of the Gulf of Siam. In October 1767, Taksin took the port of Thonburi on the west bank of Chao Phraya River. He used Thonburi as the base for defeating the Hsinbyushin's invading army and declaring himself king of Siam.

THE SINO-BURMESE CONFLICT (1765–1789)

The greatest threat to Hsinbyushin's power came from the Chinese vis-à-vis the Shan principalities who viewed Burmese incursions into the Shan plateau and the Menam valley with suspicion. The Shan principalities served as a buffer between Burma and the Chinese province of Yunnan, with Shan rulers paying tribute to one or both powers. What ostensibly began as conflict of a Shan hereditary local chieftain (saw-bwa) over suzerainty of Kengtung broke out into open warfare that engulfed the entire border region. Conflict between China and Burma was averted until December 1765, when Hsinbyushin dis-patched his armies from Ava to expel a Yunnanese expeditionary force from Kengtung and restore a Burmese-directed order. The Burmese troops were able to drive the Yunnanese forces from Kengtung back to the banks of the Mekong River, killing the Chinese commander in the process. After the Green Standard troops in Yunnan failed to capture Kengtung, the Qianlong emperor (r. ca. 1735–1795) sent his elite Manchu troops in an effort to reassert control. Despite the overwhelming military superiority the Qing dynasty was unable to defeat the Burmese. In fact, Chinese troops suffered a series of crushing defeats to the Burmese despite Chinese claims of victory.

Following a four-year campaign, a truce was reached by field command-ers of the opposing sides at the end of 1769, with the invading Qing unable to conquer the Burma. In order to maintain the status quo the Qing dynasty maintained a substantial military presence in the Yunnan border area in an attempt to wage another war. Burma and China would not establish further diplomatic contact until 1788, when they exchanged diplomatic missions. The Sino-Burmese conflict had several important consequences for Burma. First, the Burmese controlled the equilibrium of the Burma-China relationship. Second, the Burmese maintained control of the border areas, while the Shan saw-bwas adjudicated local matters. Third, it illustrated the strength of the administrative and military reforms implemented by Alaùngpayà.

6

The British Conquest of Burma

ANGLO-BURMESE RELATIONS AND THE KONBAUNG DYNASTY

British contact with the Burmese dates back to 1619 when two envoys from the British East India Company, Henry Forest and John Staveley, visited the court of Anaukhpetlun (r. ca. 1605–1628) to recover the estate of Thomas Samuel, the company's resident merchant in Chieng Mai. The East India Company would later establish commercial contacts with Burma when Thalun (r. ca. 1629–1648) granted the company permission to set up a factory at Syriam. The factory at Syriam remained in operation from 1647 until 1657. The British would continue to maintain a presence in Burma until 1740 and the outbreak of the Pegu rebellion.

The next contact between the Burmese and the British occurred in July 1756 when Alaùngpayà conquered Dagon (now Rangoon) from the Mon and discovered the presence of three British ships in the harbor. Realizing the significance of European armaments, Alaùngpayà attempted to seize the ships but was rebuffed by the English captain. Alaùngpayà's diplomatic gaffe would color later dealings with the East India Company as Anglo-Burmese relations would go from crisis to crisis.

Eager to establish relations with Alaùngpayà following his victory over the Mon, the East India Company dispatched Ensign Robert Lester as Ambassador Extraordinary to Burma in 1757, bearing a treaty of friendship and alliance between Burma and the East India Company, along with gifts of guns and gunpowder. The Treaty of Friendship and Alliance was signed on July 27, 1757, and granted the East India Company the island of Negrais and land at Bassein for factories. In return, the East India Company promised one cannon and several hundred pounds of gunpowder annually. In addition, the company promised to "aid, assist, and defend" the king of Ava and Pegu against all enemies. The treaty succeeded in promoting neither friendship nor alliance. Deeply suspicious of the intentions of the East India Company, Alaùngpayà launched a raid on the Cape Negrais settlement on October 6, 1759, massacring Captain William H. Southby and the local agents of the East India Company. The attack was in retaliation for alleged British support to the Mon rebellion of 1758. Contact between the East India Company and the Konbaung dynasty ceased in 1761 following the cessation of hostilities and would not resume until the Arakan border incidents of 1794.

THE ANNEXATION OF ARAKAN
AND ANGLO-BURMESE TENSIONS

As the British and French were occupied fighting each other across the Bay of Bengal, 35 years went by before the East India Company sent another mission to Burma. The next contact between the British and the Burmese occurred as a result of the Burmese annexation of the kingdom of Arakan in 1785 following a brief campaign led by Crown Prince Bodawpaya. This created a common border between the British and the Burmese along the Bengal-Arakan frontier. The Burmese occupation of Arakan was extremely repressive, especially in terms of the conscription of forced labor. A levy to expand the irrigation system around the town of Meiktila in 1795 set off open rebellion in Arakan, assisted by armed support of three Arakanese chiefs now living in Chittagong. The mutual distrust created by the presence of Arakanese rebels operating from within British territory created increased border tensions. Burmese troops would chase fleeing Arakanese rebels and refugees into the neighboring British Bengal claiming "the right of hot pursuit" under their own international custom, while the British denied the existence of such a right according to international law. The Burmese threatened to invade if the British failed to curtail the rebel incursions from their territory. When the Burmese commander offered to withdraw his forces if the three Arakanese chiefs were handed over, British General Erskine complied and the incident ended without further conflict.

THE RESUMPTION OF
ANGLO-BURMESE RELATIONS

Fearful of a Burmese-French alliance, the British decided to resume relations with Burma. The governor-general in India, Sir John Shore, dispatched envoy Captain Michael Symes to Ava, the capital of Burma in 1795. Symes was followed by Captain Hiram Cox in the fall of 1796. Tensions mounted as relations deteriorated when Burmese forces crossed the frontier from the Burmese province of Arakan to the British province of Bengal in pursuit of fleeing Arakanese rebels and refugees in 1799. Protracted negotiations between the Governor-General of India Marquis Wellesley and King Bodawpaya between June 1799 and June 1800 averted further conflict but failed to resolve either the Bengal-Arakan border issue or the repatriation of Arakanese refugees. Wellesley then dispatched a small British contingent to the Bengal-Arakan border and sent Symes to Burma to negotiate a full settlement.

Early in 1802, the Burmese governor of Arakan demanded the expulsion of all Arakanese refugees from Chittagong and threatened the invasion of British-held territory. Symes reached an agreement with King Bodawpaya in which the Burmese agreed not to make any more demands, threats, or incursions into the British province of Bengal but the frontier between Arakan and Bengal was never officially demarcated. This issue would later contribute to the outbreak of the first Anglo-Burmese war.

Anglo-Burmese relations were again tested in 1811 when Arakanese rebel leader Chin Byan led a rebel army across the border and attacked and defeated a Burmese garrison, eventually capturing the city of Mrohaung. Following his victory, Chin Byan extended an offer to the governor-general of India to rule Arakan under British suzerainty. While the offer was rejected by the British, the Burmese suspected the East India Company of secretly aiding and abetting Chin Byan as his bases were located well within company territory and British troops had prevented the Burmese from pursuing Chin Byan across the Naaf River boundary on the northern frontier. Eventually the Burmese crushed the rebellion, forcing Chin Byan and his rebel army to flee to the relative safety of Chittagong in British Bengal. Burmese forces again crossed the border in pursuit of Chin Byan, who managed to elude capture. The pattern of attack, followed by a tactical withdrawal across the frontier and rearmament on British-held territory would continue until 1815, when Chin Byan died. The East India Company's failure to arrest Chin Byan and his supporters while on British-held territory contributed to Burmese suspicions that the British were aiding and abetting Chin Byan and his supporters.

In 1817, turmoil at the Assamese court led Bodawpaya to send an expeditionary force into Assam in northeast India to press Burmese territorial claims. The Burmese routed the Assamese and Bodawpaya installed the pro-Burmese-Assamese Chandra Kanta Singh on the throne. The defeated Ahom princes retreated to British-held territory to recruit and arm an army. Following Bodawpaya's death in 1819, the Tai-speaking Ahom princes launched a rebellion against Burmese rule. Bagyidaw, Bodawpaya's grandson and successor, dispatched General Maha Bandula and 20,000 troops to Assam, defeated the Assamese claimants to the throne, and consolidated Burmese rule in Assam. By 1822, the Burmese army was in complete control of Assam. Following the conquest of Assam, General Maha Bandula set up a forward base of operations at Rangpur from which he could launch attacks on the British protectorates of Cachar and Jaintia in pursuit of rebels and refugees.

In 1819, the Burmese invaded the neighboring state of Manipur when Prince Marjit Singh asserted his autonomy from the Burmese court by refusing to attend the coronation of Bagyidaw. The Burmese plundered Manipur and a permanent garrison was established. Manipur became a base of operations for launching military expeditions into Assam. The Burmese army pushed west toward Assam from their garrisons along the Hukawng River. The king of Manipur and his court followers fled to the neighboring Indian state of Cachar with the Burmese army in pursuit. When the Burmese attacked Cachar, the ruler, Govind Chandra fled to British territory and requested assistance. The British acceded to this request and Cachar and Jaintia became British protectorates. The Burmese refused to recognize the British declaration and continued to cross the ill-defined Bengal-Assam border in pursuit of the rebels.

THE ORIGINS OF THE FIRST ANGLO-BURMESE WAR

The Burmese intervention in Cachar threatened the peace and stability of the frontier between Burma and British-held India. In order to prevent territorial disputes, the Governor-General Lord Amherst dispatched a detachment to Tek Naat, near the border on the Arakan frontier with another contingent stationed on the island of Shahpura, at the mouth of the Naat River. The Burmese claimed Shahpura as their territory and demanded withdrawal of the British garrison. The British refused and on September 23, 1823, a large Burmese force attacked Shahpura, killing three guards. On January 18, 1824, General Maha Bandula led two Burmese armies, one from Assam and the other from Manipur and attacked Cachar, which was under British protection. The British responded when Lord Amherst declared war on Burma on March 5, 1824, from his headquarters at Fort William in Calcutta.

THE FIRST ANGLO-BURMESE WAR

The first Anglo-Burmese war lasted nearly two years, costing the British nearly five million pounds and leading to the deaths of 15,000 British and Indian soldiers, as well as the deaths of tens of thousands of Burmese. The Burmese strategy was to capture Calcutta quickly using a two-pronged attack from Assam and Arakan, while the British planned to lure General Maha Bandula's forces from the Bengal frontier by attacking Lower Burma from both land and sea.

On May 10, 1824, Burmese forces under the command of General Maha Bandula entered Chittagong and offered to withdraw back to Arakan if the British handed over three Arakanese rebel leaders and a rebel Manipuri prince. Captain Cotton, the British commander at Ramu, rejected the offer. The Burmese attacked and routed a combined force of mixed sepoys (Indian soldiers) and a police detachment at Ramu following a battle that lasted three days.

Over the course of the summer of 1825, the British were successful in expelling the Burmese from Arakan despite the fact the Burmese defeated a British detachment at Ramu on the Arakan-Bengal frontier. In little more than a month General Joseph Morrison had conquered the province of Arakan and in the north, the Burmese were driven out of Assam. The British then launched two-front strategy using a 5,000-strong expeditionary force under the command of Major General Sir Archibald Campbell and ships under the command of Captain Charles Grant to attack Rangoon by land and by sea. The attack on Rangoon completely surprised the Burmese and the city fell on May 10, 1825, with little resistance as the Burmese inhabitants had previously fled the city.

Upon hearing that Rangoon fell to the British, General Maha Bandula led a 30,000-strong army from Arakan to retake Rangoon. But before he arrived in August General Campbell was able to attack nearby Burmese ports. On June 10, 1824, the stockades at the village of Kemmendine were attacked, forcing the Burmese to retreat further up the Ayeyarwaddy River. In late July and early August, Campbell was able to subjugate the Burmese provinces of Tavoy and Mergui as well as the coast of Tenasserim.

When General Maha Bandula did arrive he laid siege to the British positions at both Rangoon and Kemmendine. On December 7, 1824, a British counterattack broke the siege and a week later, on December 15, 1824, the British launched an attack on General Maha Bandula, which forced him to retreat up the Ayeyarwaddy River to Danubyu. Major General Sir Archibald Campbell led an advance up the Ayeyarwaddy River and on February 13, 1825, embarked on a two-pronged assault on Danubyu in pursuit of General Maha Bandula. On April 2, 1825, during the battle of Danubyu, General Maha Bandula was fatally injured by rocket fire and the Burmese army was routed. General Maha Nemyo replaced Maha Bandula and on April 25, 1825, launched an attack on the British. After several failed attacks Campbell launched his attack (November 30, 1825–December 2, 1825) and captured Prome, the capital of Lower Burma. Fighting continued until the end of 1825, when General Maha Nemyo was killed and his army destroyed. Campbell then led British forces upriver to the then capitol of Lower Burma, Yandabo, where the Burmese sought terms. Hostilities were concluded on February 24, 1826, when the Burmese signed a peace treaty.

Thus, the first Anglo-Burmese war concluded with the Treaty of Yandabo (1826) in which the Burmese ceded control of Assam, Manipur, Cachar, and Jaintia, as well as Arakan and Tenasserim, to the British. The Burmese were also forced to pay an indemnity of one million pounds sterling and accept a British resident at the Burmese court. A reciprocal commercial treaty was later signed. Despite the fact that King Bagyidaw lost almost two-fifths of his kingdom, he retained the throne.

THE CAUSES OF THE SECOND ANGLO-BURMESE WAR

The Treaty of Yandabo (1826) ended the first Anglo-Burmese war that left the British in possession of Arakan and Tenasserim and established diplomatic and commercial relations between the British and the Burmese. Over the course of the next few years a succession of protocol, border, and political issues created tension between the British and the Burmese.

By the early 1830s King Bagyidaw had descended into madness and was replaced by a regency consisting of the queen, Mè Nu, her brother, Salinmyoza, and three of the king's five brothers, princes Tharrawaddy (his full brother) and half brothers Thibaw and Kanaung, that ruled as a coalition. Behind the scenes Mè Nu and Salinmyoza schemed to gain control of the throne. Mè Nu had her brother raised to princely status and was made the de facto head of state. Mè Nu and her brother usurped control of the throne by taking control of the royal patronage network and placed their supporters throughout the kingdom. The court power struggle came to a head on February 21, 1837, when Salinmyoza ordered the arrest of Tharrawaddy's sister, the Pagan princess, on suspicion of hoarding arms. Fearing that he would be next, Tharrawaddy fled the capital to Shwebo, the seat of the Konbaung dynasty, where he gathered support and eventually raised an army. Initially opposed to open rebellion, Tharrawaddy became an instrument of his follower's discontent and their opposition to Mè Nu and her brother. Tharrawaddy's eldest daughter, a highly respected astrologer, declared the rebellion's success to be ordained in the stars.

By March 1837, Tharrawaddy had defeated the dispirited royal forces and was advancing toward Ava when several of Bagyidaw's closest advisors sued for peace. Tharrawaddy accepted the offer on the condition that the royalists hand over a list of 14 advisors. The royalists complied with the request and surrendered in early April 1837. In late April, Tharrawaddy executed the three ministers responsible for ordering the arrest of the Pagan princess. Shortly thereafter Tharrawaddy announced that Bagyidaw had abdicated the throne and his elevation to the throne.

King Tharrawaddy Min (r. ca. 1837–1845) refused to accept the terms of the Treaty of Yandabo as binding. Relations between the British and the Burmese slowly deteriorated. Successive British residents at court: Colonel Henry Burney, Colonel Richard Benson, and McLeod, allowed under the terms of the Treaty of Yandabo, were withdrawn from Burma following ill-treatment at the court. Tharrawaddy died in November 1845 and his son, Pagan Min (r. ca. 1846–1853), ascended the throne at the age of 35. Pagan Min's reign was characterized by corruption and maladministration that effected Burmese and British alike. Any thought of a thaw in British-Burmese relations were quickly dashed as British merchants in Rangoon and Ava were fined and harassed by the governor of Pegu, Maung Ok. Tired of the harassment by Maung Ok, the merchants eventually sent a petition to Governor-General Lord Dalhousie, who dispatched Commodore George Lambert to Rangoon in December 1851 to negotiate the redress of grievances and demand compensation from the Burmese. Pagan Min immediately made concessions to the British, including the ouster of the governor of Rangoon, but, for reasons unknown, Commodore Lambert provoked a naval confrontation with the Burmese by blockading the port of Rangoon and seizing Pagan Min's royal ship, thus starting the second Anglo-Burmese war.

THE SECOND ANGLO-BURMESE WAR

The second Anglo-Burmese war (April 5, 1852–January 20, 1853) led to the British annexation of Lower Burma and the gradual loss of Burmese independence.

On April 5, 1852, joint British naval and ground forces captured the port of Martaban. The city of Rangoon fell on April 12, 1852, during which the Myoza of Tabayin, a son of General Maha Bandula, was killed. After heavy fighting, the Shwedagon pagoda was occupied on April 14, 1852, when the Burmese withdrew. On May 19, 1852, the city of Bassein fell to the British. On June 3, 1852, the British had seized Pegu. By October the British had occupied Prome. Lord Dalhousie wanted Pagan Min to recognize the British conquest of Lower Burma. Following Pagan Min's rejection of peace, Dalhousie annexed Pegu on December 20, 1852, by proclamation and appointed Major Arthur Phayre as commissioner. By annexing Pegu the British were able to extend their eastern frontier to the banks of the Salween River. Pagan Min was forced to abdicate the throne on February 18, 1853, in favor of his half brother Mindon Min (r. ca. 1853–1878), who immediately sought a cessation of hostilities. As a gesture of goodwill he released all European prisoners-of-war. Mindon Min sued for peace but refused to sign a treaty ceding Burmese territory.

THE THIRD ANGLO-BURMESE WAR

The third Anglo-Burmese war was the third and last of the three wars fought between the British and the Burmese. The war ended the Konbaung dynasty in Upper Burma and saw the loss of Burma's sovereignty as Burma became part of the British Raj, a province of British India. The annexation of Upper Burma had much to do with the pressure exerted by British and other commercial interests in Rangoon.

Britain and Burma severed diplomatic relations following a succession of crises in 1879 that saw the withdrawal of British resident in Burma after the British accused the Burmese of infringing on articles of the 1862 and 1867 treaties. When the British became aware of Burmese plans with the French to purchase military equipment in May 1883, relations between Britain and Burma deteriorated further. A fine imposed on the Bombay Burmah Trading Company by a Burmese court served to trigger events that led to the British issuing an ultimatum on October 22, 1885, demanding that Burma accept a new British resident, and also included the suspension of legal action and/ or fines imposed on the Bombay Burmah Trading Company, the relinquishing of Burmese sovereignty of international relations, and the development of trade facilities in Upper Burma. Thibaw Min refused the terms on November 9, 1885, setting the stage for brief war with Britain.

In a period of two weeks between November 14, 1885, and November 27, 1885, a force of 11,000 led by Major General Harry North Dalrymple Prendergast attacked and defeated Burmese forces at Nyaung-U, Pakokku, and Myingyan, and then quickly reached Mandalay with little opposition. On October 22, 1885, British troops advanced to the Mandalay palace and demanded the unconditional surrender of Thibaw Min. On November 23, 1885, envoys of Thibaw Min offered the British terms of surrender. Thibaw Min's rule formally ended on November 29, 1885, when he abdicated the throne. Following the abdication of his throne Thibaw, his wife Supayalat, and their two daughters were exiled to Ratnagiri, India, where they lived in an official residence provided by the Indian government.

On January 1, 1886, Burma was proclaimed part of Her Majesty's dominions. While the British faced little or no resistance from the Burmese army, the British occupation of Upper Burma sparked resistance and rebellion among the populace. By mid 1886 the British were forced to send reinforcements from India as violence had spread throughout Upper Burma and most of Lower Burma. The British response to the disturbances was to shoot anyone caught possessing arms and burning entire villages. The tactics backfired on the British as villagers responded to the repression by attacking military outposts. By 1890, the British had pacified much of the resistance.

7

Burma under Colonial Rule

As the British completed the formal annexation of Burma, the consolidation of power would be swift. The king and his family were exiled to India. The early resistance against the British was in actuality armed gangs whose interest was much more inclined to gain material goods than to further any kind of political agenda. The initial colonial government made law and order the main priority.

It is difficult to overstate the impact the demise of the monarchy had on the Burmese psyche. The Burmese were a proud race with a distinctive ethnic identity and language with a shared history and territorial base. The throne was the essential element of centralization for the Burmese and this was shattered in 1885. The king's palace in Mandalay was transformed into an English club. The state had lost its cosmic character.

Any discussion of British control in Burma must address it in the context of the empire's policy over greater India. The British realized that is was in their best interest to subdue any surrounding areas perceived to be hostile and a threat to the economic well-being of the empire. The vast naval superiority of the British Empire, especially in the proximity of the Indian Ocean, helped to consolidate British regional hegemony.

The ease of British success stems from the collaboration attained from the Indian population. This partnership benefitted the indigenous population by providing jobs to build the infrastructure, employing industrial workers, and harvesting agricultural products such as rice. British capital financed this industrial development in areas such as mining, transportation, and plantations.

The British policy caused significant problems for the local Burmese population. The British had no knowledge of the Burmese and thus relied heavily on Indian assistance. Most of the wealth generated from British policy either stayed in the hands of the colonial powers or may have helped the Indian population, which was assisting the colonial administration through the influx of a professional class including bankers and businessmen. The Chettiyars, Indian moneylenders from Madras, became a dominant force in Burmese society. An Indian governing model was developed, which included taxation and land tenure. Cheap Indian labor and the importing of foreign goods further diminished the economic situation of the Burmese population. All of these policies led to intense resentment from the Burmese population. By the start of World War I, Burma was suffering significant social disorder and chaos.

Complicating the situation in Burma was the influx of immigrants into the country. A massive influx of immigrants from southeastern India and southeastern China arrived from the late-19th century through the first three decades of the 20th century. Rangoon hosted the largest Chinese population in all of Burma. The Indian population was evenly distributed with a larger percentage in Lower Burma, especially in Rangoon. By the early 1920s the majority of residents in the city were of Indian descent.

The Burmese began to associate the influx of immigrants with the British covert discriminatory policy against the indigenous population. The common notion that the British considered the Burmese too backward for equal treatment, too lazy to compete with the Indians for manual labor, and too inept to compete commercially with the Chinese exacerbated tensions with the immigrant community. The Burmese belief of exclusionary practice is born out in the fact that immigrants indeed dominated commerce, industry, and bureaucracy. The immigrant success stories throughout Burma played a significant role in attracting more immigrants to the region.

CULTURAL AND RELIGIOUS CHALLENGES

Formal education was largely shaped by a Buddhist cosmology and its cultural values. Traditionally education was rooted in the monastic mission to preserve the dharma. Scholarship and teaching were extensions of a religious vocation. Buddhist monasteries provided basic literacy for Burmese young people. Monks embodied Buddhist learning, and the monastic libraries of local communities housed the palm-leaf manuscripts that served as repositories for textual study. Monks were expected to stay removed from worldly affairs and not challenge traditional authority.

During the early colonial period, Christian schools were established first by the Portuguese and later by Roman Catholic and Baptist missionaries. Upon their arrival, the British encountered an established system of Buddhist education that had produced a high rate of literacy among the general population. Following the Anglo-Burmese war, the British government began to develop educational policies for its Indian colonies. The primary objective was secular in nature. An additional purpose was to instill an appreciation for European civilization.

Educational reform during the late-19th century greatly influenced the history of Burma. Overall colliding worldviews and political agendas defined the debate regarding education in Burma. The nationalist leaders in Burma used education to form and shape public opinion in their struggle for independence.

Monastic resistance to colonial policy increased during the 1860s when Sir Arthur Phayre proposed granting financial assistance to lay teachers in rural settings. This change led to an increase in young talent leaving the traditional Buddhist educational track. The movement to place education in secular hands was a legacy of colonialism that left a vacuum in Burmese life, for the specifically Buddhist nature of the traditional learning process was lost in the transfer to lay schools. The introduction of colonial knowledge through modern educational reforms challenged Buddhist cosmological worldviews. In a decision that proved to be a turning point in the history of education in Burma, the sangha, the Buddhist community, firmly rejected British attempts to introduce new educational subjects into the monastic curriculum.

In general, the sangha objected to the teaching of mathematics, geography, and drawing but was even more angered by the explicit government intrusion into the management and operations of the schools. The sangha feared its authority and autonomy would be compromised by cooperation with a colonial power; this refusal to collaborate with colonial authorities accelerated the decline of monastic education. This in turn fragmented an institution that had considerable power during royal times.

Between 1890 and 1910, there was a significant increase in secular schools and a concurrent decline of monastic institutions throughout Burma. This trend was especially relevant in urban areas. One side effect of this situation was that monastic education was forced into rural areas. The ultimate effect of this situation was the creation of economic, cultural, and intellectual divisions between British-educated colonial elites and Buddhist traditionalists. Ultimately, the influence of institutional Buddhism would suffer.

A major turning point in the struggle against colonial control over education came in 1916 with the emergence of the Young Men's Buddhist Association (YMBA). The purpose of the organization was to promote the reintroduction of Buddhist and Burmese subjects into the educational curriculum. The YMBA modeled itself after the Young Men's Christian Association, adopting the structure and strategies of the organization to strengthen the Buddhism in Burma.

Several monks took on key leadership roles in the struggle. The rise of U Ottama, a monk who had traveled extensively in Asia, the Middle East, and Europe, exemplified the role the sangha could play in the anticolonial struggle. His sermons stressed the decline of Buddhism under colonial rule and inspired other monks to join the nationalist movement. It is interesting to note that U Ottama was able to use print media to promote his cause even when he was imprisoned during the 1920s. His importance showed that a monk who had spent extensive time abroad and who could seem to be disconnected from his homeland could be a leading figure in the struggle against the British. As with his role model Gandhi, U Ottama would be imprisoned on three different occasions during his civil disobedience campaigns. His encouragement of economic self-reliance and boycotting helped to steer the nationalist path in a positive direction.

Initially the YMBA was not in direct opposition to colonial policies. The membership of the group consisted of mostly young, British-educated colonial elites. The goal was centered on enhancing the national spirit and emphasizing Burmese culture, literature, and language, as well as Buddhism. The organization did have a more modern and rational perspective on promoting Buddhism. The emergence of the group was a result of the fragmentation of the sangha. Initially the group played a part in providing a welfare function and helped to coordinate the work of several Buddhist organizations. The function of the group was as much civic as religious. The educational outlook encouraged both religion and modernity.

Eventually the YMBA became the cornerstone of patriotic grassroots work in Burma. In part, the group's focus became somewhat reactionary as more Burmese became disenchanted with modern society. Many Burmese also felt a loss of national identity that the YMBA seemed to connect to. The YMBA did champion a more significant role for lay people regarding religious authority. This message was appealing to Burmese who were emerging middle class, modern, and Buddhist. The initial support the group received from colonial authorities soon dissipated. The group sought to impact the morality of society by condemning intoxicants and in general immoral behavior.

Following World War I, Burmese nationalism accelerated as the YMBA recreated itself as the General Council of Burman Associations, or GCBA. The leaders of the organization were not monks or professors, but English-trained lawyers. By 1920, student protests exploded in Burma. Sir Reginald Craddock, the lieutenant governor of Burma proposed creating Rangoon University. The structure of the university would be modeled after the American Baptist and Rangoon Colleges, which in general terms was elitist with only the wealthy being admitted. The students demanded admission based on ability and the curriculum being broadened. The Burmese students wanted a modern educational system developed, which would in turn further the goals of the nationalist cause.

FACTIONALISM WITHIN THE NATIONALIST MOVEMENT

Within a few years the unity of the GCBA was fractured. Followers of U Chit Hlaing wanted a type of "home rule" where Burma would be completely divorced from India and given a much greater degree of autonomy. Eventually this would in turn lead to full independence. The minority position championed by U Ba Pe urged continued unity with India in the hopes that the nationalist gains of the much better organized Indian National Congress would trickle down to the Burmese nationalists. This would expedite independence. The "home rule" concept was the majority position within the nationalist movement.

A major issue driving this wedge was dyarchy. The British implemented this concept because of the realization that the colony could not be governable in the long term. The British in India officially introduced dyarchy in 1919. Because Burma was part of the colony, several executive council positions were reserved for the Burmese. Dyarchy introduced some of the concepts of democracy to the colony, including enfranchisement of all adults aged 18 and older, including women. This was a liberal concept for the time.

EMERGENCE OF BURMESE NATIONALISM

Several issues connected to World War I helped to intensify nationalism within Burma. Shipping shortages disrupted the rice-export trade causing unrest within the population. Furthermore, several poor growing seasons also exacerbated the tension within Burma. In addition, Burmese citizens were angered by tax assessments that they did not comprehend. These economic issues in turn caused social and political unrest.

A political turning point for Burma as well as for the entire developing world was President Woodrow Wilson's statement concerning self-determination for the colonized populations globally. This coupled with the growing trends in India toward nationalism helped to spark a political awakening within Burma. Indigenous products were driven out of the market and local manufacturers were eventually out of business. The traditional economic structure was either diminished or lost entirely. The Indian model provided structure and procedures for the Burmese nationalists to follow.

The starting point for the nationalist movement in 20th-century Burma was an incident during 1916–1917 concerning the prohibition of the wearing of shoes on pagoda premises. A lawyer and YMBA member by the name of U Thein Maung found a sign at the Shwe Sandaw pagoda that read, "No one permitted to wear shoes in this pagoda but Englishmen and Asiatic Europeans." The fact that European visitors to pagodas generally did not remove their shoes was sacrilegious behavior in the eyes of many Burmese Buddhists. This belief was rooted in ritual practices of traditional, cosmological Buddhism. This action was considered desecration of sacred space. The sign was replaced with one stating that footwear was banned for everyone. The matter led to a tense dispute between colonial authorities and the emerging YMBA. The organization passed resolutions stating that foreign companies could not use the Buddha and pagodas in their trade or brand marks. Furthermore, the group would forbid the wearing of footwear in religious places. The British perceived this to now be a political matter, which they claimed the YMBA had no right to engage in. Thein Maung's action transformed a religious matter into one that ultimately was anticolonial and nationalist.

The shoe question indirectly led to a rift and factionalization within the Burmese nationalist cause. The older members wanted to take a more moderate conciliatory path working within the system to push for change. The younger members wanted changes in orientation and strategy, which they believed would empower the nationalist cause.

A TURNING POINT IN THE NATIONALIST STRUGGLE: THE HSAYA SAN REBELLION OF 1930–1931

Multiple rebellions had broken out in early 20th-century Burma. In 1910, petty cultivators took up arms in Sagaing, Shwebo, and Chindwin districts. A few years later, the authorities faced upheaval in the Mayoka uprising. In the late 1920s, an insurrection emergence occurred in the Tharrawaddy area.

San, a former medical practitioner and teacher, was born into a rural family in independent Burma in 1879. His early career focused on urging Burmese peasants to rely on traditional medicines rather than the expensive Western remedies. He published several works outlining his ideas on his preference for traditional Burmese medical practices. During his travels, he observed the crushing poverty that the majority of Burmese peasants suffered. He eventually joined the GCBA, being put in charge of a research project dealing with British policies in rural areas. The focus was on the collection of taxes and the ill-treatment of Burmese peasants at the hands of British authorities. San promoted the idea of a "people's volunteers" to oppose colonial authorities, which was considered too radical for the mainstream of Burmese activists. San believed the only alternative was armed insurrection.

The decision to actually take up arms may have been accelerated because of the deepening economic troubles related to the global depression. Market prices were in sharp decline and peasants' request for a postponement of tax collection was denied. San's charismatic appeal and forceful rhetoric probably helped to further promote the cause.

San used secret societies and traditional symbolism to promote the rebellion. The galon, a mythical bird, became the main rallying symbol for the resistance. The colonial opposition was referred to as nagas or snakes. The resistance army tattooed with the galon and a secret oath would be sworn. Many of San's followers used amulets and charms that they believed made them impervious from bullets. San proclaimed the capital at Alan Taung (renaming it Buddha Raja).

The rebels attacked government outposts in the Tharrawaddy area, but ultimately spread elsewhere. San's forces were poorly armed in comparison to the seasoned colonial fighters. The British called in reinforcements from India as San's army rapidly fell apart. Not only were casualties mounting from the fighting, but they also were decimated by disease.

San was forced to flee to the northern Shan state in a futile attempt to ferment rebellion among some of the ethnic minorities. In August, San was captured and over a period of several months the remaining resistance forces were destroyed. A special tribunal was established and convicted San, who was executed in December 1931. San became a martyr for Burmese nationalism. The movement fueled the fire of nationalism and put the vernacular press in a more active role. The harsh response from the British authorities played into the hands of nationalist agitators.

Overall, the rebellion was the result of the interaction of various factors, including political ferment, national consciousness, economic distress, opposition to taxation, and racial bias against foreigners. The momentum created by the insurrection heightened tensions as well as providing momentum for additional nationalist movements. The British were now forced to pay closer attention to the situation in Burma. Ultimately a new breed of younger nationalists known as the Thakin emerged on the scene.

NATIONALISM: POST SAN REBELLION

An urban response to the Hsaya San rebellion emerged through a group known as the Dobama Asiayone (We Burmans Association). Ultimately the group referred to its members as Thakin or master. The rationale behind the name was that the growing number of Burmese insisted that the population must take on a master mentality and discard the slave mentality that resulted from colonialism.

The Thakins used the setting of Rangoon University to promote the cause of Burmese nationalism. As the global depression worsened and discontent over educational policy continued, the Thakins stock continued to rise. The Rangoon University Student Union was the main organization in which the group aired their grievances and provided a forum for nationalist aspirations. The initial leaders included Maung Nu and Aung San, both who would play central roles in the independence movement in Burma. Student strikes occurred in 1936 that ultimately spread beyond the confines of the university. Many of the student activities quickly became full-time political operatives.

Ideologically, the Thakins were leftist leaning, inspired by the Fabian socialists from Britain. Some of the key leaders also drew inspiration from Sun Yat Sen's Chinese nationalism, as well as Gandhi's independence movement and the Irish Sinn Fein. The Thakins were some of the first advocates for total independence from Britain. Unlike earlier nationalist movements centered on religion, the Thakin cause was more secular in orientation. Some within the movement wanted to draw on Buddhist concepts in combination with Marxism ideology.

It was apparent to the colonial authorities that the situation in Burma was tenuous at best. The British authorities announced the Simon Commission Report and the Burma Round Table Conference. The commission recommended that Burma should be separated from British India. The final legislation entitled the India Act of 1935 (also called the Government of Burma Act) officially separated the two entities and promulgated a new constitution for Burma.

A new government structure was established for Burma that included the governor remaining in charge of the executive along with a 10-member council of ministers. The legislative branch was expanded to two houses; a senate with 36 members and a house with 132 members.

MINORITY PROBLEMS IN COLONIAL BURMA

The economic problems in colonial Burma exacerbated tensions between the indigenous Burman population and the sizeable minority population within the colony. In urban centers such as Rangoon, immigrants arrived from southeastern India and southeastern China. Many immigrants would go back and forth between Burma and their home country. Opportunities in Rangoon led to a large influx of immigrants in the early part of the 20th century. Over 50 percent of Rangoon's population in 1921 was from India. The presence of these groups stirred resentment especially as nationalist fervor was emerging by the 1920s and 1930s. The colonial administrators considered the Burmese unfit to be governed. They were stereotyped as lazy and incompetent. Their educational levels were lowered, leading to a British policy of using the Indians for administrative duties. Furthermore, both the Chinese and Indian populations were heavily involved in commerce and money lending, especially in the urban centers.

THE ECONOMIC SITUATION IN COLONIAL BURMA

Colonialism significantly impacted traditional Burmese economic relationships. The economic situation in precolonial Burma was loosely structured with considerable power situated at the village level. The village head was the point of connection between the peasants and the state. The relationship between the head and peasantry was symbolic. The head provided assistance during times of need or during celebration and ceremonies. The peasant in turn provided needed labor and possibly military assistance.

By the mid-19th century, a large rice-exporting economy was developing in Lower Burma. The growth of the rice export economy (a 600% increase occurred in the late-19th century) led to massive migration from the north. Thousands of northern peasants resettled in the delta from 1870 to 1910.

The political changes connected with colonialism would impact economic and social relations. The village head could no longer be the protector of the peasantry. The agrarian population was much more vulnerable to poor harvests and the overdependence upon a single crop. Furthermore, the colonial administration would not prove to be as flexible as the village head had been traditionally. The British policy was geared toward generating enough revenue to pay for the colonial administration of Burma. Tax collection was very structured and this led to the economic dislocation and land alienation, especially in times of hardship. Numerous impoverished peasants would end up defaulting on loans and ultimately lose their land. This also led to exploitation by moneylender immigrants from India known as Chettiyars.

The Burmese population felt that the British did not attempt to mitigate the situation, causing further frustration within the peasant communities. One of the initial responses from the Burmese was the formation of village associations to protect the interest of the peasants. The associations did not trust the colonial authorities and called for boycotts as well as social pressure to help the nationalist cause. Citizens were discouraged from collaborating with the colonial authorities through campaigns of intimidation and ostracization. These decisions led to harsh reprisals from the colonial administration. The police presence was increased and numerous groups were outlawed.

The anticolonial nationalistic struggle impacted every aspect of Burmese society. The economic and social structure of Burma was forever changed. The issue of minority relations as well as Buddhism played a significant role in the nationalist movement. As with most anticolonial struggles, political concepts from the West helped to shape the direction of the particular movements. Factional struggles at times hindered the advancement of the agenda. The issue of whether to take a more traditional or modern direction in the struggle was central for several decades. Ultimately, the Japanese helped to settle the question with their actions in Asia. The modern and more secular Thakin faction would carry the movement through World War II.

8

The Japanese Conquest of Burma

THE OUTBREAK OF WAR

Even though Japanese expansion into Asia began in 1931 with the invasion of Manchuria and continued in 1937 with attacks throughout northern China, it wasn't until 1942 that the Japanese Imperial Army (IJA) invaded Lower Burma, aided in part by General Aung San and the Thirty Comrades and their Burma Independence Army (BIA). Japan's interest in Burma was a result of the recently completed, strategically important Burma Road to China. If the Japanese were able to close the Burma Road, they would close the Allies' only land supply route into China. The Japanese could also use Burma to defend their recently conquered Southeast Asian territories.

The Japanese took Burma with astonishing speed and ease. On December 11, 1941, Japanese aircraft bombed the airfields at Tavoy, south of Rangoon. The next day Japanese troops infiltrated the Burmese border and skirmished with British and Burmese troops. They were followed by units of the BIA, who provided logistical and intelligence support, including the collection of food and resources in the newly occupied areas, the gathering of intelligence from villagers, and the sabotage of British operations. The Japanese launched a full-scale invasion of Burma on January 20, 1942, when the 55th Division of the

Southern Expeditionary Army crossed the Thai-Burma frontier at Tanintharyi with Moulwein as their immediate objective. Further north, the 33rd Division began advancing along established jungle tracks toward the Salween River. Using a series of fast outflanking moves the 55th Division quickly defeated the 16th Indian Infantry Brigade at Kawkareik and on January 31, 1942, the Southern Expeditionary Army captured Moulwein after the 7th Burma Rifles disintegrated and large-scale desertions affected other units. The Seventeenth Indian Light Division, comprised the 16th and 48th Indian Infantry Brigades, fell back behind the Salween River to protect Rangoon, where it was reinforced by the 46th Infantry Brigade. The Japanese Fifteenth Army's 143rd Regiment crossed the Salween River on February 8, 1942, and built a roadblock on the Martaban-Thaton Road. The next day the Japanese attacked and captured Martaban. Further north the 33rd Division attacked and defeated the 7th/10th Baluch Regiment on February 11–12, 1942, forcing the withdrawal of the 46th Infantry Brigade to Rangoon. The loss of two brigades meant that Rangoon could not be defended. General Harold Alexander, the recently appointed commander of the Burma Army, ordered the city of Rangoon to be evacuated after the port and oil refinery had been destroyed to prevent capture by the Japanese. As the British began their retreat north from Rangoon they destroyed much of Burma's infrastructure, including rail lines, river boats, and communication networks to prevent them from being used by the Japanese.

THE RETREAT FROM RANGOON

After the fall of Rangoon, the IJA reorganized and began an offensive designed to pacify Upper Burma. The 55th Division followed the route to Toungoo, while the 33rd Division went up the Ayeyarwaddy valley toward Prome. By the middle of March, the 55th Division, aided by the BIA, had inflicted a heavy defeat on the Seventeenth Indian Light Division at the Sittang Bridge, cutting off several British and Indian units before they could be pulled back across the Sittang River. The Japanese were then able to seize Pegu, cutting railroad links leading north out of Rangoon. In the Ayeyarwaddy valley, the 33rd Division pushed past Prome toward the oil fields at Yenangyaung. On April 14, 1942, retreating British and Indian forces set the oil field ablaze to prevent them from falling into Japanese hands.

After reaching Toungoo Japanese forces divided into two columns, the 55th Division continuing northward toward Mandalay, while the 18th Division made a flanking move along the Mawchi-Loikaw Road. By mid April, the 18th Division dislodged the Chinese from the area around Loikow. This left the entire left flank of Allied forces exposed. There was little chance that the poorly armed British, Indian, and Burmese forces could continue to hold their lines. The remainder of the campaign was a rout. In fact, there was the real chance that Allied forces would be isolated and annihilated by the advancing Japanese Army. On May 1, 1942, Mandalay fell. The escape of these Allied forces was essential for the defense of India. The only escape route for Allied troops and civilian refugees was a 600-mile trek through jungles, over rivers, and across mountain ranges. The exodus of troops and refugees was complicated by the fact that over 90 percent of the participants had contracted malaria.

The allied defeat in Burma was mainly due to the reliance on insufficient air and naval power combined with ill-equipped and poorly trained infantry units. Trucks and tanks left the allies dependent on roads, while the lightly armed Japanese took to the jungle, quickly outflanking and enveloping the allies. Profound disagreements over military strategy, including whether or not to defend Mandalay in Upper Burma or to counterattack Rangoon contributed to the loss of Burma.

THE STRATEGIC IMPORTANCE OF THE BURMA ROAD

The term "Burma Road" is actually a misnomer. In actuality, the Burma Road was a 1,154-kilometer supply route comprising a series of roads and trails built by the Allies and completed in 1939, linking Lashio, in eastern Burma, to Kunming in Yunnan province, China, to supply Chiang Kai-shek's nationalist troops. Both the Allies and the Japanese realized the strategic importance of the Burma Road. If the Allies were able to keep the road open they would be able to continue an overland supply route to the nationalist Chinese troops, thus enabling the Chinese to keep open a vital front against the Japanese. If the Japanese were to succeed in closing the Burma Road, they would force the Allies to fly supplies via northwest India over the Himalayas to continue to supplying the Chinese. Keeping the Burma Road open was not only important militarily, but also psychologically for the Allies. The IJA had swept through Southeast Asia conquering all in front of them. Reputations were won and lost as a series of Allied commanders came to terms with the Japanese and the dense Burmese jungles. Men such as Lieutenant General William Slim, General Joseph Stilwell, and General Orde Wingate would become household names in the United States and Great Britain for their exploits against the Japanese in the jungles of Burma.

Following the invasion of Manchuria in 1937, the Japanese set about cutting off supplies to the Chinese. In June 1940, Japanese warships moved into French Indochina and closed the railroad at Haiphong. A short time later the Japanese secured British acquiescence to close the Burma Road. The British reopened the Burma Road in October 1940 and for a time it was the only route to supply nationalist Chinese troops fighting the Japanese along the eastern seaboard of China. If the Japanese were to close the Burma Road they would be able to blockade China. Without Allied assistance China's would not have the ability to oppose the IJA.

CONSOLIDATING CONTROL OVER BURMA AND THE CREATION OF THE BURMA AREA ARMY

Following the conquest of Burma, the Japanese spent the next two years familiarizing themselves with the geographic and climatic conditions of Burma. During this period, from late 1942 to early 1943, the Allies mounted two counteroffensives in an attempt dislodge the Japanese from Arakan. The first was an advance into coastal Arakan where the Indian "Eastern Army" led by Major General Wilfred Lloyd planned to reoccupy the Mayu Peninsula and adjacent Akyab Islands, which controlled access to the mouths of the Mayu River and the Kaladan River, the major rivers into the Arakan. Control and possession of the Akyab Islands was strategically important for the defense of Rangoon as well as potentially serving as a gateway for the Japanese to attack India.

Initially, the Allied offensive met with success. The 14th Indian Division quickly occupied the port of Maungdaw and the town of Buthidaung. The village of Indin was quickly occupied. Following their initial success, the Japanese were able to inflict heavy losses on British and Indian troops at Donbaik-Laungchaung on the Mayu Peninsula and at Rathedaung on the eastern bank of the Mayu River. The Japanese began a counteroffensive when reinforcements from central Burma flanked Allied positions by crossing the supposedly impenetrable Mayu mountain range. The Japanese were able to cut off advanced British troops and soon took the village of Indin. The Allies believed the Japanese would then try to capture the Maungdaw-Buthidaung Road. The Allies planned to encircle the Japanese but when a British battalion gave way the Japanese were able to take the Maungdaw-Buthidaung. Despite mounting several counterattacks, Allied troops in Buthidaung and the Kalapanzin valley were cut off. On May 11, 1943, the Allied offensive ended with British and Indian troops retreating to India. Despite having overwhelming numerical superiority, better artillery, as well as a monopoly in tanks, the offensive ended in complete failure. A second Allied offensive into Arakan fared better. Allied troops were able to capture the port of Maungdaw. Before the Allies could launch another offensive, the Japanese 55th Division counterattacked. Unlike the first Arakan offensive, the Allies stood firm and were able to inflict heavy casualties on the Japanese. The offensive came to an end at the onset of the monsoon season.

The threat of further Allied offensives from India forced the Japanese to strengthen their forces in Burma. On March 27, 1943, three Japanese armies—the 33rd Army in Upper Burma, the 15th Army in central Burma, and the 28th Army in the south—were consolidated into the Burma Area Army (BAA). The BAA was then tasked with the mission to defend Burma. In May 1943, the 54th and 55th Divisions were formed in Japan and then transferred to Burma under the command of the BAA. In January 1944, the 2nd Division left the Solomon Islands and was reconstituted in Burma as the 28th Army with the 24th Brigade. In April 1944, the Imperial General Headquarters (IGHQ) in Japan activated the 33rd Army to defend Upper Burma. The 56th Division, the 18th Division, the 53rd Division, and a part of the 49th Division were incorporated into the newly created 33rd Army.

THE TURNING POINT—THE BATTLES
OF KOHIMA AND IMPHAL

The Japanese did not originally have plans to advance into Assam and invade India at the onset of World War II, but Lieutenant General Renya Mutaguchi convinced the Japanese Minister of War, Hideki Tojo, that the only way to eliminate the Allied aerial threat to Burma was to control northeastern India. This would create a buffer zone between India and Burma. By controlling northeast India, the Japanese could then cut off the Allies aerial supply route over the Himalayas to China, thereby completely cutting off all Allied supply operations to China.

General Mutaguchi's invasion plan was originally rejected by his superiors. Mutaguchi's plan "Operation U (U-Go)" was eventually approved by the Southern Expeditionary Army in Singapore and the IGHQ in Tokyo. The key to the planned offensive was to gain control of the strategically important Imphal plain. If the Japanese could take control of the city of Imphal they could control access to plain in which an invading army would have to cross. Mutaguchi also planned a simultaneous attack on town of Kohima to cut off the British and Indian supply route to Imphal. If the Japanese could take Kohima ridge they could control the only road that led to the Allied supply depot at Dimapur leading to Imphal. Mutaguchi's plan was to use speed and surprise to encircle and destroy the numerically superior forward-deployed Indian troops at Torbung, Tamu, and Palel leading to Imphal. Once the Japanese captured Imphal they would secure much-needed provisions and munitions to sustain the momentum of their offensive.

The Indian IV Corp was responsible for the defense of Imphal. When the Japanese attacked, the British and Indian troops attempted to engage the Japanese on the plains near Imphal, forcing the Japanese to fight with an extended supply line. Unfortunately, the Allied commander reacted too late to lure the Japanese into a premature engagement. The Japanese offensive began on March 8, 1944, but the order to fall back to Imphal wasn't issued until five days later on March 13, 1944. As a result, Indian supply dumps and ordinance depots in the Chin Hills were captured by the Japanese and in the process they became encircled. The 214th Regiment of the 17th Division successfully counterattacked at Tuitum saddle on March 18, 1944, allowing the 17th Division to recover their supplies and safely retreat to Imphal on April 4, 1944. The Japanese pursued the withdrawing Indian troops. Once the Indian 17th Division reached Imphal, the Japanese attack began. The Japanese 33rd Division moved up the Kabow valley from their base in Tamu and attacked from Bishenpur. Units from both the 15th and 33rd Divisions then attacked Shenam saddle near Imphal, only to be stopped by the Indian troops. From the north, the Japanese attacked and captured the supply dump near the town of Kangpokpi and then captured Nungshigum Hill. The Japanese had anticipated that following the initial phase of their offensive, the Allies would retreat under pressure. Instead the Allies took positions along the roads on a 90-mile arc from Kanglatombi and Kameng, Shenam, and Bishenpur in the south. Unlike previous engagements the Allies withstood the initial Japanese onslaught and were able to coax the Japanese into fighting a battle of attrition. Unable to secure provisions at Imphal the Japanese were faced with the prospect of fighting a prolonged campaign with an extended supply line through the dense Burmese jungles.

After Imphal was attacked, a near-simultaneous attack on Kohima began. On April 5, 1944, the Japanese 31st Division attacked Kohima ridge. Initially, the First Assam Regiment set up defensive positions east of Kohima before being forced withdraw to more isolated positions along Kohima ridge. Reinforcements from 161st Indian Brigade, Fifth Indian Division, and the Fourth Royal West Kents took up defensive positions in and around Kohima. On April 7, 1944, additional Allied reinforcements arrived from Jotsoma. The Allies were able to contain initial Japanese advances and combat turned into a stalemate. The Japanese laid siege to Kohima beginning April 8, 1944, forcing the Allies to supply the defenders by air. On April 10, 1944, the Japanese were able to force the Kohima garrison to withdraw. By April 13, 1944, the Japanese sought to press their advantage against Allied positions by attacking positions along the Kohima ridge. The attack was eventually repulsed by British artillery from Jotsoma. The next day the Japanese responded with artillery barrages against Kohima and Jotsoma garrisons but withheld launching a ground offensive. The failure to launch a ground attack gave the British 2nd Division time to arrive on April 15, 1944, after breaking the Japanese roadblock on the Dimapur-Kohima Road. The arrival of fresh troops relieved the beleaguered Indian 161st Brigade. The Japanese launched a final desperate assault on the evening of April 16, 1944. Heavy fighting ensued.

By May 1, 1944, Indian troops stabilized their lines and were reinforced by the 33rd Brigade of the Indian 7th Division on May 4, 1944. Although the Japanese lines, were tough to break down, their supply situation had become critical. The situation took a turn for the worse on May 12, 1944, when the Indian 114th Brigade arrived. The XXXIII Corps attacked southward from Kohima toward Imphal. Japanese troops fought back against the British and Indian attack. Nevertheless, the Japanese troops were driven from area surrounding Kohima at the end of May. By May 25, 1944, the Japanese troops were short of both food and supplies. On May 31, 1944, Japanese troops withdrew from Naga Hills.

The XXXIII Corps was then joined by IV Corps in attacking the Japanese along the Dimapur-Imphal Road on June 22, 1944. When British and Indian troops took milestone 109 the siege of Imphal was lifted. The Japanese 33rd Division was reinforced by battalions from the 53rd and 54th Divisions. The Japanese continued to press their attack on Indian troops despite previous setbacks. The Japanese came close to penetrating the Indian lines at Bishenpur, but suffered high casualties, which ended the offensive on July 3, 1944. The defeats at Imphal and Kohima are the largest defeats in Japanese military history. The Japanese suffered over 55,000 wounded with 13,500 killed.

THE BEGINNING OF THE END— THE HUKAWNG CAMPAIGN

The Allies main priority in the Burma theatre was to reopen the supply route to China. The Hukawng campaign had multiple objectives: to cut the Allied supply route connecting India and China, to provide flank protection for the Imphal operation, and to capture a large number or Allied troops. U.S. trained and equipped Chinese divisions and smaller American units advanced into Hukawng at the end of the monsoon season in November 1943, ostensibly to reopen the Burma Road. At the time of the Allied advance Japanese units in Upper Burma had assumed a defensive posture to support offensives against India.

The battle for Hukawng began in early 1944 when the Japanese 18th Division advanced westward toward Ledo across the Hukawng valley. The operation was designed to forestall the Allied offensive in the west of Kamaing and to engage as many Chinese and American forces as possible. In February 1944, the 1st and 6th armies under the command of Lieutenant General Joseph W. Stilwell as well as "Merrill's Marauders," part of the 6th Airborne Division gradually pushed the Japanese 18th Division to retreat to Myitkyina. Strategically, Myitkyina was important in the Burma theatre. If the Allies could take Myitkyina, they could isolate Japanese forces between Hukawng and Yunnan fronts, as well as open the way for the Allies to threaten Mandalay.

THE BATTLE FOR MYITKYINA

The Allies captured the railway leading to Myitkyina on March 10, 1944. In late April 1944, the Chinese launched an attack from Yunnan. Japanese forces in Upper Burma were easily defeated. The Allied offensive against Myitkyina began on May 17, 1944, when airborne glider troops under British General Orde Wingate landed behind Japanese lines at Myitkyina airfield. The Allies were able to take airfield with relative ease, but were unable advance further because of stiff Japanese resistance. On June 3, 1944, the 42nd and 150th Chinese Regiments attacked Myitkyina and suffered heavy casualties. Over the next month, a battle of attrition combined with exhaustion and disease claimed a significant number of casualties on both sides. The Japanese garrison held out until early August. After seeing the main part of his army safely withdraw, General Mizukami committed suicide. This allowed other Japanese troops time to prepare a defensive line further south. On August 4, 1944, Myitkyina was finally captured. The capture of Myitkyina allowed the Allies the use of key airfields.

After the Allies had regrouped after the capture of Myitkyina, they pushed south again. At this stage of the Burma campaign Japanese strategy changed to a defensive posture in hopes of holding on to southern Burma, abandoning their plan of maintaining a northern flank to threaten the allied supply line to China.

THE END OF JAPANESE OCCUPATION

The battle of Myitkyina marked the beginning of the end for the Japanese suzerainty over Burma. The Allies continued their campaign in Burma in late 1944 and early 1945. In Arakan, the XV Corp launched an assault on Akyab Island. Unable to halt the Allied advance the Japanese retreated from Akyab Island on December 31, 1944. The XV Corp then launched an amphibious assault on the Myebon Peninsula on January 12, 1945; 10 days later, the Allies cut off the retreating Japanese. Fighting lasted until the end of January when the heavy casualties suffered by the Japanese limited their ability to put up an adequate fight. The XV Corp went on to capture Ramree Island and Cheduba Island, giving the Allies control over southern Burma. In Upper Burma, the 14th Army, consisting of the IV Corp and the XXXIII Corp, led the main assault. The IV Corp mission was to cross the Ayeyarwaddy River at Pakokku and seize the Japanese communication center at Meiktila, while XXXIII Corps continued to advance toward Mandalay. By February 1945, the XXXIII Corps had seized control of the crossings over the Ayeyarwaddy near Mandalay. In late February, the 7th Indian Division captured the crossing at Nyaung-U near Pakokku. The 17th Indian Division and the 255th Indian Armored Brigade then attacked the Japanese garrison at Meiktila. The Japanese tried to relieve their garrison and, after failing, tried to recapture the town itself. After suffering heavy casualties and losing most of their artillery pieces Meiktila eventually fell on March 1, 1945. Following the loss of Meiktila the Japanese retreated further south to Pyawbwe.

Following their success in Upper Burma, the XXXIII Corp launched a dual-pronged assault down the Ayeyarwaddy River valley against the Japanese 28th Army. The IV Corp led the main assault on the "railway valley" followed by the Sittang River. The IV Corp were held by remnants of the Japanese 33rd Army at Pyawbwe until a flanking move by the Allies caught the Japanese by surprise and broke their defensive lines. From this point, the Allied advance to Rangoon faced little organized opposition from the Japanese. An uprising by Karen guerillas prevented the reconstituted Japanese 15th Army reaching Toungoo before the IV Corp captured it. The Japanese 105th Independent Mixed Brigade made a last stand 40 miles north of Rangoon on April 25, 1945, and held out April 30, 1945, allowing for the evacuation of Rangoon. On May 1, 1945, a Gurkha battalion cleared the Japanese rearguard from the mouth of the Rangoon River and Rangoon was liberated on May 22, 1945.

Following the fall of Rangoon the Japanese put up scattered resistance. In Arakan the Japanese 28th Army had retreated to the Pegu Yomas, where they hoped to break out and join the BAA. Miscommunication between the Japanese 28th Army and the 33rd Army led to the 33rd mounting their attack two weeks before the 28th Army was ready to break out. The break out was a failure. In all, the Japanese lost nearly 10,000 men. This effectively was the last campaign in the Burma theatre. Japanese forces in Burma surrendered on September 13, 1945.

9

From Independence to Military Dictatorship: Burma 1948–1962

The modern history of Burma emerges with the completion of independence from Great Britain. The elections of April 1947 solidified the Anti-Fascist People's Freedom League (AFPFL) as the legitimate party to lead Burmese independence. The Constituent Assembly declared that Burma should be an independent republic with key constitutional guarantees of social, political, and economic justice. Furthermore, all power was to emanate from the people and minority rights were to be safeguarded. The tragic assassination of national hero General Aung San along with six cabinet members on July 19, 1947, did not derail the independence process.

POLITICS IN BURMA: 1948–1958

On January 4, 1948, at 4:20 A.M., the independent Union of Burma came into existence. Prime Minister U Nu took over a fragile state. Members of the AFPFL would dominate Burmese politics during this initial decade. U Nu was considered to be an inept leader who lacked the administrative abilities as well as the charisma of Aung San. Early electoral success could not conceal the troubling turmoil brewing in Burma. Multiple problems, including the issue of federalism, as well as civil wars based on ethnic and ideological lines, would haunt early Burmese independence. Furthermore, external threats from powerful neighbors prompted the military to take an early and significant role in Burmese society. U Nu appointed General Ne Win to several cabinet posts, as both the military and police presence increased substantially in the postindependence period.

The new Burmese political system was unitary. Multiple ethnic groups felt uneasy in a Burman-dominated political system. Alienated Karens, Shans, Kachins, Chins, Mons, and Arakanese clamored for more autonomy within the separate regions. Fractures occurred throughout the 1950s as the Karens, Mons, and Arakans created separate states. The structure originally established was complicated as the Shan and Karenni were allowed to secede after 10 years but that same right was denied to other ethnic groups. Citizenship rights were limited to people belonging to any of Burma's indigenous groups or with ancestors born in Burma and inhabiting Burmese territory for at least two generations. These measures particularly affected Burma's Chinese, Indian, and Muslim Rohingya populations.

Burma's government was a parliamentary democracy. The president had limited power and was indirectly elected by parliament. The legislature, or Pyithu Hluttaw, was a bicameral system. The lower chamber of deputies was elected by universal suffrage, while the upper chamber of nationalities was divided by ethnic minorities and representatives from territories ruled by the central government. Particular ethnic minority leaders were guaranteed representation in the lower chamber.

The AFPFL dominated the political situation in Myanmar from 1948 to 1958. This control was a legacy of the organization's association with the anticolonial struggle. Many of the early leaders were philosophically socialist, but in the Burmese context this was considerably watered down. Different factions within AFPFL used a patron-client relationship in order to sustain loyalty to the party.

The AFPFL won overwhelming victories in the first two general elections, winning 147 of 239 contested seats. U Nu's rise as the leader following the death of Aung San can be attributed to his honesty and knowledge of the government structure. He seemed determined to end widespread corruption, which led to him gaining significant support in both rural and urban areas.

ECONOMIC POLICY IN POSTINDEPENDENT BURMA

U Nu launched a four-year plan to convert Myanmar into a welfare state. The goals included improvements in education, public health, subsidized housing, easy credit, and debt relief. In addition, U Nu promoted the reallocation of several million acres of farmland to new tenants. The early emphasis of the economic program was rural projects rather than industrialization.

Additionally, the issues confronting the newly independent Burmese state included nationalization, industrial development, and land reform. Burma's leaders were committed to altering the nation from an agrarian rice-based export economy to a balance between agriculture and industry. The newly independent state was trying to transform Burma using its own financial, intellectual, and technical resources. Financial shortcomings led to an overreliance on the sale of rice to support the new economic sectors. U Nu's goal was a welfare state that would be fiercely independent. The overwhelming burden for economic development fell on the government.

Burma depended on the individual farmer to make key decisions concerning the technical side of agriculture. The state was present to facilitate the lending process and the marketing of the rice. Ultimately the state was the owner of the land, even though the private sector controlled key decision making. From the technological aspect, Burma was backward. Simple plows, water buffalos, and natural fertilizers were still used, keeping output down. Burma did not fare well in comparison to other nations within the region. The government through the State Agricultural Marketing Board (SAMB) purchased the product at a low fixed rate and quality control was not taken into account.

During the Korean War, global demand for rice increased, which helped the Burmese economy. Following this period, demand fell sharply and the notoriously poor quality of Burmese rice lead to a marked decline. The problem at times was with the state because the government did not encourage the farmers to cultivate a higher-quality product. The vast majority of peasant farmers were conservative by nature. Ultimately, the basic farmer wanted little beyond what he grew and, most of all, to be left alone by government and insurgents.

Foreign entrepreneurs and business firms heavily populated Burma's business sector. This sector looked abroad for Western models that would help develop the economy. However, the government was beset with corruption and mismanagement, which hurt the development of this sector of the economy.

Eventually the SAMB, which was responsible for marketing of Burmese rice, was proven to be unreliable. They did not keep up with inventory, and did not know the condition of the product or the market fluctuations. Ultimately, the state had to turn to outside assistance.

The socialist states became the main trading partners, but this required a barter-like system. The Burmese state ended up accepting low-quality goods in exchange for the rice. Eventually the United States established a trade arrangement with Burma so that products such as powdered milk, tobacco, and cottons could be purchased.

The Burmese industrial sector was a disappointment. Investment was not well developed and methods and equipment were labor intensive and aging. Furthermore, Burma did not have skilled managers and technicians to establish a solid industrial economy. Finally, poor transportation and power systems and the lack of raw materials spelled doom for industrial development in Burma.

One of the essential ways to make up for deficiencies in the Burma economy was to enhance the educational system of the nation. Under U Nu, Burma promoted rapid increase in educational spending, which expanded the number of schools and teachers. Furthermore, the state sent candidates abroad for additional training. The two areas where the system was most deficient in was the lack of trained candidates as well as adequate facilities.

The overall goal of Burma from the time of independence was to achieve socialism. The initial two-year plan called for land redistribution, restoration of the agricultural sector to prewar prominence, self-sufficiency; nationalization of particular industries; and emphasis on state ownership. The insurgency problem slowed the progress toward socialism, especially in the first three to four years following independence.

Following advice from the United States Economic Cooperation Administration, Burma invested heavily in both the private and public sectors. The United States sent in engineers and economists to help in the development of an eight-year plan. With an overly ambitious goal of a 31 percent in GNP increase over the prewar period, Burma seemed to be facing a serious economic challenge. The goals of the plan were not met, as rising prices and failure to meet targets led Burma to take loans out to help in capital development. Ultimately, Burma could not transform a backward agrarian society into a modern state with a balanced economy.

By mid 1957, U Nu admitted that numerous mistakes had been made in the initial plans to form a socialist economic system. Consequences of these early blunders included a lack of a coherent production plan for materials being ordered; preordering of machinery that was delivered prior to having a place to house it; a flawed accounting system to calculate a cost-benefit analysis. The role of the caretaker government under Ne Win would alter the economy in significant ways.

THE ROLE OF BUDDHISM
IN POSTINDEPENDENT BURMA

U Nu was a devote Buddhist who wanted to create a bridge between religion and the state. Burmese scholars believe that U Nu may have moved in a more religious direction publicly after the split with the more leftist elements within Burma. The concept of nationalism through Buddhism may have been appealing to many within the governing elite in Burma.

Michael Charney, author of *A History of Burma*, believes three variables impacted Nu's decision to adapt a more public advocacy of Buddhism. First, Nu sincerely believed in the concept of merit being vital to a Buddhist society. Second, monks were becoming much more politically active in the post–World War II period. Many monks pushed for a designation of Buddhism as the official state religion. Finally, Buddhism was a way to counter the growth of radical communism in Burma (Charney 88–90).

The push for Buddhism began with the state attempting to control the structure and function of faith within society. The Vinasaya Act of 1949 dealt with monastic infractions as well as registering and monitoring behavior. Furthermore, U Nu set up Buddhist universities and encouraged missionary activities. Finally, the World Peace pagoda was constructed as well as the large man-made cave known as the Maha Pasana Guha. Nu went to the extreme of hosting and promoting the Sixth World Buddhist Council, which commemorated the 2,500th anniversary of the Buddha's attainment of nirvana. The hosting of the council may have actually resurrected the idea of making Buddhism the state religion of Burma.

U Nu's Buddhist philosophy may have impeded him from taking action at times. The Buddhist prohibition against doing harm was something that Nu took seriously. This factor made dealing with opponents in a firm way difficult. Buddhist philosophy may have also played into his decision to take a neutralist route in foreign policy.

On a personal level, U Nu was involved in grassroots efforts to promote Buddhism. He restored pagodas, liberated animals, cleansed Buddha images, and sponsored religious ceremonies. Nu even took time off from his position as prime minister to meditate at holy places or monasteries.

The issue of religion, however, was a volatile one. With Muslim, Christian, and animist minority populations, U Nu had to walk a tightrope in dealing with the issue of religion and the state. The Buddha Sasana Council Act provided a way to enforce the government's policies in dealing Buddhism. The Buddha Sasana Council pushed for the resumption of Buddhist religious instruction in state schools and the formation of an inquiry committee to deal with non-Buddhist religious instruction in schools as well. When Nu took steps to ensure the teaching of religions other than Buddhism, such as Christianity and Islam, in the schools, monks blocked these efforts. Nu encouraged the monks and lay protesters to view religion and politics separately. Interestingly enough, Nu would use Buddhism as a way to expel communists from the political process.

The decision to proclaim Buddhism as the official Burmese state religion was delayed for several years. The military was still secular in nature and was facing numerous insurgencies that were non-Buddhist. The fact that Ne Win and others did not want to exacerbate the tension was practical in a time of civil war. It was also the desire of Burma's founding father Aung San to keep a more secular outline in state religious affairs.

THE ROLE OF THE MILITARY (TATMADAW) IN BURMA

By the time of independence in 1948 the Burmese military was seriously factionalized. This would decimate the military for the first two years of independence. The same issues that divided Burmese politics hampered the military. The ethnic divisions as well as ideological disagreements and the issue of power distribution made cooperation problematic.

The ultimate result of these initial problems was a military that was dominated by small state-armed villages, towns, and district militias organized by party leaders. This localized control spelled problems for the development of national identity in the Burmese state. The citizens did not have confidence in the government's ability to protect them. Further hampering efforts was the fact that desertion levels were high in the period from 1948 to 1950.

From 1950 to 1953, the tatmadaw laid the foundation for its eventual consolidation of authority within the state. According to Myanmar military expert Mary Callahan, author of *Making Enemies: War and State Building in Burma*, the expanding institutional clout of the military was a result of the decades-long struggles over how power would be constituted, by whom, and in whose name, and across what territory. Furthermore, the external threat from the KMT (Chinese Nationalist Party) helped the military push for additional funding and training. Many within Myanmar started to look to the military and the leaders within Burma. Civilian politicians did not seem to get the job done, especially in dealing with external threats such as the China insurgency. Slowly but surely, law and order returned to the Burmese countryside. The state ultimately became reliant on army field commanders, warlords, and militia leaders to gain access to the population. The citizens also saw the military as the only way to gain access to the state. Thus, the military played a sort of "middleman" role in Myanmar.

Following Ne Win's promotion to commander and chief of the armed forces in 1949, the Burmese military began an extensive expansion and improvement. As the military bureaucracy in Burma gained strength, substantial increases were seen in funding for training, equipment, and support. Furthermore, the Defense Service Institute became heavily involved in the economic sector. This led to the military having enormous control over the import-export business in Burma. The growing clout of the military widened an earlier rift between civilian politicians and army leaders such as Ne Win and Aung Gyi.

The fact that Burma faced so many threats in the postindependence period set the stage for military dominance in political affairs. War fighters became state builders, according to Callahan. The military would be responsible for resource allocation, centralization of the state, and expansion of territory. Confidence was lost in the civilian government as more and more of the time citizens and the government itself turned to the military for solutions.

CIVIL STRIFE IN POSTINDEPENDENT BURMA

Endemic conflict between the majority Burman government and ethnic minorities threatened the political progress of Burma. The country has a complicated cultural and linguistic structure. Two-thirds of Burma's 52 million people are Burman, while the rest is made up of multiple ethnic minorities. The ethnic groups are distinguished in terms of language, culture, and religion.

In the early years of the Myanmar republic multiple insurrections occurred, stifling the development of the nation state. Insurgencies emerged from both political and ethnic factions. The first groups to launch insurrections included the Karen, Mon, and Arakanese groups. Within five years the Shan and Kachin armies launched further insurrections. Finally, the Chin-armed rebellion has been a constant problem for state authorities.

The most significant problem facing the Burmese state was the civil war between the communist movement and the newly formed state of Myanmar led by U Nu. The communist movement in Myanmar split into two factions. The moderate and larger "White Flags," or Burmese Communist Party (BCP), were led by Than Tun, while the smaller and more radical "Red Flags," or CPB, were led by Thakin Soe.

The issue of weapons proliferation exacerbated the insurgency problem in Burma. Most groups had weapons that were left over from the British withdrawal in the early 1940s or the Japanese departure in 1945. Furthermore, the Burmese resistance had an ample supply of arms from the allies during the latter stages of the conflict.

The British decision to rule the CPB illegal prior to granting Burma independence was the actual spark that started the insurrection, according to Charney (61). Both communist movements appealed to the peasantry with popular platforms of land redistribution and poverty alleviation. U Nu's regime considered bringing the more moderate "White Flags" into the government fold but ultimately the lack of trust between the parties doomed any potential deal. Within the first year of independence, U Nu was unsuccessful in his attempt to arrest the communist leadership, ultimately leading to full-scale civil war.

U Nu felt that building a coalition with members of the People's Volunteer Organization (PVO) along with socialist and moderate communist party members was the best plan to create stability in Burma. Ultimately, the co-alition plan faltered as factions of the PVO decided to rebel.

THE KAREN INSURGENCY

The Karen situation was unique compared to other minority populations in Burma. The Karens were a tribal group that migrated from China in the seventh century. Nationalism within the Karen community is tied to Christianity, which sets the group apart from the majority Buddhist in Burma. Furthermore, the Karen population had suffered abuse at times under the Burmese monarchy. By the late-19th century, Karen nationalism was readily apparent with the formation of the National Karen Association. The Karens decided to work with the British colonizers. Following brutal treatment during the Japanese occupation, Karen leaders clamored for a separate Karen state.

The relationship between the Karens and Burman were aggravated during the period of British colonial rule. Following independence this distrust only worsened. The Karen leadership believed that the British had promised the Karens an independent state. The decision was made to boycott the Constitutional Assembly elections scheduled for 1947. Tension was high at the time of Aung San's assassination in July 1947. The Karen were led by Saw Ba U Gyi. The formal or official break occurred during the meeting at Moulmein in late 1947. The group demanded complete separation and a sizeable independent state for the Karen population. Justin Windle, author of *Perfect Hostage: A Life of Aung San Suu Kyi, Burma's Prisoner of Conscience,* states that Saw Ba U Gyi expressed the four key demands of the Karens: "There shall be no surrender; recognition of a Karen state must be secured; the Karen's shall always retain their own arms; the Karen's must decide their own political destiny." (184). The AFPFL rejected the Karen National Union's proposal for a separate state.

The Karen position was problematic. The Karen population is not monolith; numerous factions both religiously and politically were apparent. A Karen state would have been vulnerable to external powers. Finally, a Karen state would have been difficult to sustain economically.

The advantages of the Karen insurgency were numerous. The Karen National Liberation Army was well trained by the British and also had sufficient weapons. The anarchy ensuing in Burma made the timing for an insurrection practical. With numerous insurgencies emerging from both ethnic and political organizations, the Karen leadership felt a sense of confidence during the 1947–1949 period.

The clear starting date for the actual insurrection is disputed. Some historians cite the rebellion starting in the summer of 1948. The Palaw massacre in Tenasserim in December 1948, in which 80 Karen peasants were slaughtered, clearly increased the tension level. Other sources mark the 1949 battle of Insein as the beginning point.

By early 1949, the tide seemed to be turning in the Karen direction. An alliance with communist rebels led to the capture of Mandalay. During the summer, much of the countryside was under rebel control. The Karen forces, bolstered by desertions from the Burmese military, may have outnumbered government forces three to one. Lieutenant General Ne Win replaced the Burmese military chief, a Karen named Smith-Dun. Making matters worst, the Karen success led to increased rebel activities from ethnic groups, as well as communist supporters boosted by Mao Zedong's success in the Chinese civil war in 1949.

The Karen movement suffered from factionalization, which seriously damaged the insurgency at a critical time. Karen sympathy for communism, while being a predominately Christian group, was troubling at times. The Cold War proxy situation in Southeast Asia probably hurt the unity of Karen nationalism as members of the movement became engulfed in the drug operations in the Golden Triangle region. Finally, alliances between the different insurgency groups were always temporary as the Burmese state was able to divide and conquer at appropriate times.

ADDITIONAL ETHNIC ISSUES

In addition to the Karen problem, the Burmese regime encountered difficulties in dealing with the Shan, Arakanese, Chin, and Kachin populations. Aung San's savvy political maneuvering in dealing with minority leaders helped to keep the peace at least temporarily. Many ethnic leaders did not see an advantage in being part of the newly forming Burmese state. The Panglong Agreement of 1947 temporarily calmed the ethnic problem by promising a Kachin state in the north, as well as autonomy for the Shan minority. The Chins were promised significant aid, which guaranteed their agreement to join the Union.

As chaos spread in Burma, Naw Sang, a Kachin commander, forged an alliance with the Karen in 1949. During the early months of 1949, the insurgency peaked, capturing Mandalay. However, by the fall the tide had turned in favor of the government forces. The lack of coordination and trust between ethnic groups allowed the Burmese military to successfully regroup under Ne Win. Though the rebellion lasted for several years, the initial gains made were not sustained.

THE CHINA PROBLEM

On October 1, 1949, Mao Zedong formally proclaimed the People's Republic of China, ending a decades-long civil war. Remnants of Chiang Kai-shek's nationalist forces crossed from Yunnan province into the Burma's Shan states. The initial wave of deserters, led by General Li Mi, crossed the border and did not threaten the stability in the Shan areas. The following year, a larger and more organized force of KMT soldiers entered Kengtung. The Guomindang forces enlisted local Shans and tribes to increase their strength. Eventually the Guomindang forces received extensive aid from Taipei and also covertly from the United States. With the subsequent conflict in Korea, the Burmese state worried about the real possibility of a communist Chinese invasion. The Guomindang forces moved family members to the region, intent on settling in for the long haul.

Further complicating matters, the Guomindang became heavily involved in the Southeast Asia opium trade. After U Nu pleaded with the United Nations for assistance, pressure was put on Taiwan to withdraw from Burma. The Guomindang forces were now becoming local insurgents with the main priority being the lucrative drug trade. Hundreds of forces remained behind, however, for the next several decades. The task of cleaning out the Guomindang fell on the Burmese military under Ne Win. The success of the military operations gave the fledging military much-needed legitimacy. From the Burmese perspective, this was a wake-up call to create a bigger and better army. High-ranking members of the Burmese military were sent aboard for study and training in areas such as Israel, Yugoslavia, and Western Europe.

Eventually, the United States backed the Burmese military action against the Guomindang. The United States realized that Burma's neutrality in the Cold War took precedent over a futile attempt to prop up an insurgency that had no real chance of making significant progress against the People's Liberation Army in China. The neutrality of Burma was enhanced by U Nu's role in the Bandung Conference of 1955, which formulated the Non-Aligned Movement.

DEMOCRATIC PROGRESS AND REGRESSION: 1956–1962

The 1956 elections were dominated by the AFPFL. The National United Front was dealt an embarrassing defeat. U Nu decided to step down as prime minister for one year as he attempted to reunite the party. Ba Swe took over the temporary helm of the party with an agenda to restore law and order to Burma. U Nu returned as prime minister in February 1957, but the AFPFL was fractured beyond repair.

The AFPFL split in 1958 over the issue was both institutional and personal, according to historian Charney. The legacy of Aung San was wearing off nearly a decade after his assassination. The insurgency upheaval and rebellions probably helped to keep the party together for longer than it would have under different circumstances. The internal tension was heightened following the suppression of the insurgency movements. U Nu and Thakin Tin led the "clean" AFPFL faction. Kyaw Nyein and Ba Swe led the "stable" faction. The stable faction was actually the larger group because of the backing from the socialist in Burma. U Nu countered the growing support for the stable faction by pardoning prisoners, opening the door to greater autonomy for states, and legalizing outlawed movements such as the communist party. Political and military organizations chose sides, leading to intense bickering and infighting. The situation worsened, turning violent during August and September. After talks with military commanders Maung Maung and Aung Gyi, Nu made the decision to hand over the reigns to the military so that a caretaker government could be temporarily formed under the leadership of General Ne Win.

U Nu encouraged the population to put their faith in Ne Win, who promised that free elections would be held within six months. The rationale behind this decision was based on the belief that stability and order would be restored with the general in charge. This would supposedly make the democratic transition easier to accomplish.

THE CARETAKER PERIOD: 1958–1960

The primary task of the caretaker government was to restore law and order to Myanmar, no matter what the consequences were to the freedoms and liberties of the population. Hundreds of arrests were made and numerous rebel groups were beaten into submission. Ne Win also oversaw a bureaucratic reorganization in towns and villages. Civilian politicians and party politicians were removed from positions of power and replaced by civil servants and individuals with connections to the armed forces. Interestingly enough, the army was not directly involved in politics, but their role was to be administrative in nature. The reality was that the military entered government buildings and police stations, set up roadblocks throughout the cities, and checked for hidden weapons caches.

Many Burmese citizens believed that a coup had taken place. A number of weeks passed before the situation was clear to most people. U Nu claimed that power was transferred to avoid bloodshed and possible foreign intervention. Student groups and other organizations fearful of military suppression staged protests against the change.

The new Burmese administration pushed for a dramatic overhaul of the administration. Bureaucracy mismanagement and endemic corruption plagued

Burmese politics. The essential key to changing the system was to get input from the population; clear communication challenges were vital. The National Solidarity Associations (NSA) were formed throughout the country, with the goal of creating democracy on a grassroots level. This in turn would build confidence in the system, leading to economic growth. The work of the NSA was in several ways to be above the political fray. Party politics was seriously frowned upon. The military also took it upon itself to reform organized labor in Burma, making unions more grassroots and less top down. This infusion of new leadership would also lead to more confidence in the political system.

The most successful policy of the caretaker government was the "sweat" campaign. Started in late 1958, the campaign's goal was to instill civic pride and public responsibility in the citizens of Burma. Tun Sein led this massive clean-up effort, which would take place every Sunday. Members of the government, armed forces, and the public were involved in what became known as "Operation Clean-Up." The Burmese government received assistance from the U.S. International Cooperation Administration in order to help with sewage and water supply problems. Infrastructural problems such as street repair and widening were addressed. Citizens were discouraged from chewing betel, which is spit out, leaving a messy residue on the walkways and streets.

The caretaker administration also encouraged the Burmese citizens to adopt good manners and teachers were to tighten discipline in the schools. A national registration system was also implemented in order to facilitate more law and order in society. Hundreds of rebels were killed or captured; many surrendered during this period. Ethnic minority and tribal leaders were either bought off or forced to surrender. Many administrative positions were now in the hands of the military rather than civilians. Crime did indeed drop during the 1959–1960 period.

Economic decision making by the military was increased during the caretaker period. General Aung Gyi took more direct control over economic policy. The Defense Service Institute increased its control over factories, shipping, and banking. Essentially the military was perceived as making sound judgments concerning economic policy. The fact that the military government seemed above the political fray (e.g., the military never formed a political party) helped it retain its legitimacy.

THE FINAL PHASE OF DEMOCRACY
IN BURMA: 1960–1962

Parliamentary elections were held in February 1960 to return Burma to civilian rule. U Nu ran as head of the clean AFPFL, which focused his campaign on promoting Buddhism as the state religion and the possibility of increased federalism, which would benefit the ethnic minority populations. Nearly 60 percent of the population voted, making it the most successful elections in Burmese history. U Nu's had an overwhelming victory and his two main rivals Ba Swe and Kyaw Nyein both lost their seats. U Nu renamed his party the Pyidaungsu Party (Union Party). Borrowing from some of the popular themes of General Ne Win, U Nu implemented further governmental reform at the local level and a promise was made that the new Burmese democracy would be grassroots in nature.

U Nu's policies were met with opposition and ultimately factionalization reemerged. The Pyidaungsu movement was dysfunctional and Burma seemed on the verge of chaos. Economic problems were returning and U Nu announced the nationalization of foreign trade on March 1, 1962. This alienated the business community, as the legitimacy of the regime was in question. The issue that truly ended Burmese democracy was the federalism dilemma. U Nu was in discussions to grant greater autonomy to the Shan leaders. The idea of rewriting the constitution to create a true federalist system was in the works. National unity seemed to be dissolving, leading to Ne Win and the military to take action that would forever change the history of Burma.

10

Myanmar 1962–1988:
The Dictatorship of Ne Win

In the early morning hours of March 2, 1962, mechanized units of the Burmese military moved into Rangoon and secured control of all governmental structures, including the courts, legislative buildings, the airport, telegraph office, and police stations. Key leaders of the government, including Prime Minister U Nu, were arrested, along with multiple government ministers and the chief justice of the Supreme Court. Included in the round up were Shan, Kachin, Kayak, and Karen leaders. For the most part, the coup d'état was bloodless and efficient.

The rationale behind the action was the deteriorating condition of the union, according to Ne Win. The parliament was disbanded and the constitution suspended. The Revolutionary Council was quickly assembled within 24 hours following the coup. Members of the council were connected to Ne Win as far back as the anticolonial struggle of the 1930s–1940s. The council included Aung Gyi, Tin Pe, San Yu, and Sein Win. Ne Win was named minister of defense, finance, and revenue. Furthermore, he became president of the republics. No mention was made about future elections.

The federalism dilemma, especially in regard to the Shan states, was the decisive issue that destroyed Burmese democracy. In critiquing the problems of the U Nu regime, the Revolutionary Council stressed multiple issues. Projects that did not directly impact the population were scrapped. For example, the new national theater was demolished and renovations to the parliament building were stopped. Emphasis was given to the development of agricultural infrastructure, such as fertilizer, water pipes, and insecticides. The religion issue so prominent during the latter U Nu years was abandoned in place of more freedom of religion and religious tolerance. Finally, the Revolutionary Council proclaimed freedom of the press.

Several weeks after the coup, the Revolutionary Council announced the government plan that was to be known as the "Burmese Way to Socialism." The focus of the document was both social and economic. Popular participation would be encouraged and a high priority was placed on guaranteeing the basic necessities, such as food, security, shelter, and clothing. The rhetoric of the document was egalitarian with an emphasis on narrowing the income gap and promoting unity.

In order to foster national cohesiveness, the Revolutionary Council decided that a single-party state would be established. The legacy of the Anti-Fascist People's Freedom League (AFPFL) infighting of the late 1950s played into this decision. After the main parties failed to merge, the Burmese Socialist Party (BSP) was established. Representatives from the Pyidaungsu Party, the AFPFL, and the National United Front were told that assets would be seized, including the forfeiting of all property. Continuation of political activity not associated with the BSP would lead to jail time. The goal of the party was nation building and the ideology borrowed from Marxism as the guiding principle was to be "democratic centralism."

One of the early targets of the Revolutionary Council was civil liberty. The government at first claimed that civil liberties would be preserved as long as they did not threaten the security of the state. An especially problematic area was press freedom. The regime felt that a supportive media was essential to build nationalism and loyalty to the state. The media could help slow down the moral decay of the colonial and early postcolonial years. Within the first two years of the new regime, horse racing was banned, and dance halls and ballet schools were closed.

The xenophobic nature of the regime was exemplified with the treatment of the press. Foreign coverage was to be tightly controlled. The New Agency Burma was established to control international media coverage. This was a step toward eliminating an independent media. Additionally, the government could control press credentials to ensure that only pro-government journalists were in the field. The mindset of the regime was that the press was there to serve the population and promote patriotism. Furthermore, the press should be cautious and avoid sensationalism and any attempts to sabotage government programs. The press was to strongly back the "Burmese Way to Socialism." In many ways, Ne Win's Burma resembled the communist states of Eastern Europe in how the media was controlled and manipulated.

STUDENT PROTEST AND
GOVERNMENT RESPONSE

The main target of the Revolutionary Council would be the well-organized student movement in Burma. The universities were the hotbed of activity against the state, as well as the place where future political leaders would emerge. Any opposition to the state would lead to the closing of the school system from a few days up to several months. This could, of course, have severe repercussions for the economic development of Burma as well as the morale of the citizens. University councils were disbanded because of excessive foreign influence in educational policy and administration.

The military would take control over the universities in both Rangoon and Mandalay. After curfews were set by the military and hostels were closed, student activists took action. The Rangoon University Student Union, staged protests and took control over the student union. By the next morning, the military asserted control and blew up the union building. The building was historically significant because Aung San and the Thirty Comrades had organized themselves at that location back in the 1930s. The university would remain closed for the next four months.

Many historians believe any chance of Ne Win acquiring popular support for the regime was fatally damaged by blowing up this symbol of the anticolonial struggle that was closely associated with the national hero Aung San. The military was now heading down a different path, one in which its legitimacy was not guaranteed. Later, Ne Win attempted to blame subordinates for the action, but the damaged was already done.

The Revolutionary Council also wanted to separate religion from politics. Monastic orders that tended to be more conservative and less political won the favor of the new administration. Ne Win wanted to clearly articulate the importance of freedom of religion in order to distance himself from the previous administration under U Nu. The regime was walking a tightrope between alienating the Buddhist majority while at the same time wanting to secure its Buddhist credentials. A process of weeding out false or politically active monks was implemented in 1964. The Buddha Sasana Sangha Organization was formed in an attempt to control Buddhist activity in Burma. By the following year, Ne Win would move against monastic autonomy and attempt to nationalize the sangha. Hundreds of monks were arrested for engaging in antigovernment activities. Furthermore, Baptist and Catholic missionary activities had ceased because any remaining missionaries were forced out by the mid-1960s. By all indications, the Revolutionary Council was trying to assert control over independent religious activities. When challenged or threatened by the religious hierarchy, the council took a hard-line stance that would be the order of the day in Burma for the foreseeable future.

FOREIGN POLICY AND THE INSURGENCY ISSUE

An additional goal of the new government was to rid the country of foreign influence. Ne Win was believed to harbor intense animosity toward foreigners, especially Indians. The Indian community had been reduced during World War II. Ne Win implemented anti-Indian policies in 1964, forcing thousands of citizens out of the country. Many families had been in Burma for generations. They spoke Burmese and were an integral part of the social and cultural landscape. No compensation was given to the Indian population when 400,000 Indian citizens were forcibly removed. Vibrant members of the Burmese community such as doctors, lawyers, shopkeepers, businessmen, and teachers left en masse. This xenophobic action harmed not only the Burmese economy, but also the society in general. Burma did not suffer any significant backlash from the Indian state, which took in many of the individuals as refugees.

The China-Burma relationship was somewhat more complicated. During U Nu's tenure, the People's Republic of China (PRC) stayed neutral, refusing to give any significant support to the communist insurgency in Burma. Peking had actually been a key leader in the Non-Aligned Movement formed at Bandung in 1955. The PRC actually renounced any connections with the Burmese communist movement. With the emergence of the Revolutionary Council, the policy regarding the communist insurgents was bound to change.

The PRC was become radicalized as Peking launched attacks against Moscow and against any communist movements that they considered "reactionary." The Chinese branded the Revolutionary Council reactionary, and Beijing even labeled Ne Win as a Chiang Kai-shek of Burma. The ouster of pro-PRC Aung Gyi as a key policymaker in Burma put an additional strain on the relationship. With the onset of the Cultural Revolution in China, the Burma-China rift widened.

Internally, the Burmese Communist Party (BCP) was split along a Moscow-Peking divide. The BCP under Than Tun followed a Maoist model and took base in Pegu Hills. Burmese Red Guard units were established. Harsh reprisals against anyone suspected of having sympathy toward Moscow were implemented. Mass trials and purges of what was labeled "Moscow returnees" took place. Most disturbing, Buddhist temples were targeted and monks were assassinated. This extremism led to an implosion of the BCP.

Within Burma, the Chinese community had their own schools, and most were loyal to the PRC government. Many within the community showed support for Mao and the Cultural Revolution. When the Burmese economy started to decline, the Chinese became a convenient target for the disgruntled unemployed youth in Burma. Riots occurred and Chinese businesses were looted and burned. The Burmese authorities allowed this communal violence to occur so that the focus would be removed from the failing policies of the Revolutionary Council.

At the peak of this altercation, China launched an incursion into Burmese territory, attacking a garrison at Mongko. Initially the Chinese forces were successful, as 3,000 miles of territory was seized by the summer of 1968. Ne Win now turned to both Moscow and Washington for help. A limited amount of assistance came from the United States in the form of weapons and equipment and some training for air force pilots. The USSR sent in an advisory team and discussion of aid accelerated.

The Burmese military quickly rebounded. First they dealt with the internal problem of the BCP. The BCP forces were isolated and could not get needed aid and supplies. Ne Win's forces assassinated the party chairman Thakin Than and the BCP base was overrun within days. As the Cultural Revolution died down, support for the incursion into Burma lessened. Ultimately the forces that stayed behind worked with the Shan insurgents and dealt mostly in the drug trade for the next several decades. They did not pose a serious threat to Ne Win's regime.

Internally the Revolutionary Council granted a blanket amnesty to anyone willing to lay down his or her arms. Initial talks held with multiple insurgent groups bore little fruit. Following the communist implosion of the late 1960s, the Burmese authorities had to contend with a Shan insurgency on the border with Thailand. The growing drug trade in the notorious Golden Triangle of Southeast Asia may explain the growth of this movement. The geographic isolation of the region and the logistical difficulties of formulating a logical counterinsurgency campaign worsened the problem. Attempts to form local militias to combat the insurgents were disastrous, as groups such at the Ka Kwe Ye were driven only by the goal of maximizing profits. The massive corruption within the region triggered by the lucrative profits from the drug trade help to explain the longevity of this movement.

The most successful attempt at forging an antigovernment insurgency was the National Democratic Front (NDF) formed in 1974. Included in this coalition were the Karen National Union, as well as the Arakan, Kachin, and Kayan insurgency factions. As with earlier coalitions, the NDF was beset with a lack of coordination as well as the absence of external support. The movement did agree to a common goal of a federal system unlike earlier attempts to create independent nation-states, which was unrealistic at this time.

The Karens were the main faction member and were unable to sustain any momentum. Tacit support from Thailand ended by the late 1970s. Furthermore, the Burmese military launched successful incursions against the Karen's during the mid-1980s. Not only did this offensive hurt the military strength of the Karens, but it also economically cut off the group from essential revenues near the border.

ECONOMIC POLICY 1962–1988

Unquestionably the most significant internal rife in Burma during the Ne Win regime was in dealing with economic policy. Aung Gyi, who had organized the economic restructuring during the caretaker period, was initially in charge of economic decision making following the coup. Aung Gyi's faction wanted industrialization and a slow approach to nationalization. The private sector would be permitted to continue in industry and the import-export sector would be allowed to continue. Foreign investment would be encouraged, while the import substitution industrialization program, which started during the caretaker period, continued. The emphasis early on would be small industry.

Tin Pe, a former minister of mines, labor, public works, and national housing, led the main opposition faction in the post-1962 period. Pe emerged as the minister of cooperatives and agriculture and forests following the Revolutionary Council's takeover. Tin Pe called for a more radical Marxist approach to economic policy. The cooperative held the key to the "Burmese Way to Socialism" and the government needed to aggressively implement cooperative efforts. The radical faction pushed for greater emphasis on crop rotation, paddy transplantation, and the use of high-quality seeds.

Both the USSR and United States were helpful in these agricultural endeavors. The Soviets would be instrumental in the construction of dams for irrigation. The Burmese government would be required to hire Soviet engineers and contract only through the USSR for the upkeep and needed machinery. The United States through the United States Agency for International Development (USAID) loaned the Burmese government 3.4 million dollars to assist in land reclamation in the Ayeyarwaddy and Pegu regions. The staunch neutrality of the Burmese government (even dating back to the U Nu period) probably helped to facilitate these agreements with the Cold War rivals.

The plan for Burma's economic future was laid out with the issuing of the "System of Correlation of Man and His Environment" in early 1963. This document was a strange ideological mix of Buddhism, Marxism, and historical dialecticism. According to the document, the exploitation of man by man should be discouraged. Man should be responsible for the spiritual growth of society and class antagonisms should be abolished. Society was always in flux so the leaders in Burma needed to be willing and able to alter the plans accordingly.

By mid 1963, the radicals led by Tin Pe had won the fight and would determine Burma's economic policy for the foreseeable future. Aung Gyi resigned from the government and would later be detained by the authorities. Any members of the government or military that had supported Aung Gyi were removed from their posts. Many experts believed that under Te Pin's stewardship Burma was heading toward communism. The role played by Ne Win in the economic decision making taken in Myanmar at this time is unclear.

One of the top priorities of Tin Pe's plan was rapid nationalization of all sectors of the economy. Banking as well as factories and export trade were all nationalized. The "Tenancy Law Amending Law" was passed in 1965, which freed peasants from obligations to landlords. The state control over the economy continued to increase with the passage of the "Law Empowering Action in Furtherance of the Construction of the Socialist Economic System of 1965." The state had a near-total monopoly over the means of production.

Opposition to these economic policy changes quickly occurred. The shortage of consumer goods and the emergence of a thriving black market played into this discontent. Burma was no longer a significant exporter of rice. Loan defaults were on the rise and a general lack of confidence in the economic system was apparent.

With the economic turmoil engulfing Myanmar, Ne Win decided to rehabilitate Aung Gyi. Over the next two years Gyi's influence increased, while Tin Pe was forced into a subservient role until his eventual retirement in 1970. The damage done by the economic mismanagement of Tin Pe would not be easily countered.

In the early 1970s, steps were taken to introduce free-market concepts into Burma. Once government rice quotas were met, the extra amount could be sold on the open market. Government prices were well below the free market, leading to minimal delivery to the government. Prices remained high and the population in general was frustrated and angry at the authorities.

Labor unrest spread, and rail workers and several state facilities went on strike. The authorities used excessive force to suppress the workers on several occasions. According to Michael Charney in *A History of Modern Burma,* the labor problems were based on four factors: factories were build in a haphazard fashion; the government's ignorance of the growing discontent; the preoccupation with reforming the constitution at the expense of dealing with other problems; and outside subversion which threatened to destabilize the state (137).

By the late 1970s the Burmese economy was in shambles. The xenophobia and isolation of the BSP caused considerable long-term damage to the economy. The regime was going into heavy debt. World Bank members set up a common policy for aid distribution to Burma to no avail. China also started to heavily fund the regime. As the debt doubled and exports were cut by over 50 percent, the regime reacted by devaluing currency. The corruption and black market also strangled any economic development efforts. Burma was classified as a least-developed nation by 1987. The debt had reached 4 billion dollars and GDP targets goals were not met.

DOMESTIC TURMOIL

Because of insurgency and economic problems, Ne Win decided to build a stronger domestic coalition. By 1969, Ne Win had released most of the former governmental leaders incarcerated following the 1962 coup d'état. Even though the former officials U Nu, Ba Swe, and Kyaw Nyein pledged not to participate directly in politics, Ne Win asked them to serve on a new advisory board to facilitate the writing of a new constitution for Burma. Ne Win's rationale was based on the belief that bringing the former members of the regime into the government, even in an advisory position, would give the Revolutionary Council needed legitimacy. The Internal Unity Advisory Board was formed to facilitate the constitutional revision and strengthen national unity.

U Nu pushed for the return of civil liberties and a semblance of authentic democracy to Burma. The Revolutionary Council quickly became concerned about the potential of U Nu rebuilding a popular base. Nu was spending most of his time touring the countryside and lecturing about Buddhism.

In 1969, U Nu was granted permission to travel aboard and he quickly turned on the Burmese government. The Parliamentary Democracy Party was proclaimed in August 1969 with the goal of peacefully overthrowing the Ne Win regime. If the party were not allowed to operate on Burmese soil, the alternative would be armed insurrection. The threat was perceived as legitimate since U Nu embarked on a global tour of prominent countries. Even more threatening was the decision of numerous disgruntled groups to form the United National Liberation Front coalition led by U Nu, to forcibly oppose the Revolutionary Council.

The antigovernment alliance quickly disintegrated. In general, the coalition lacked any sort of organizational base. Furthermore, strong rivalries emerged among the different leaders of the factions. Numerous operational failures, including a commando raid to steal supplies and ammunition, failed miserably. By the late 1960s, the Burmese military was a well-financed, well-trained fighting force that could soundly defeat the insurgent forces. A final blow to the resistance movement came when U Nu was asked by the Thai authorities to leave the country. Without the base of operation in Thailand, the movement was doomed.

The Revolutionary Council decided to officially formulate a political party that would mirror the goals of the "Burmese Way to Socialism" and thus formed the Burma Socialist Program Party (BSPP) in 1971. It took almost a decade for the military dictatorship to form a political movement that would be open to mass membership. The goals of the party included drafting a new constitution and a return to civilian rule. Input from the population was encouraged. The process would be painfully time consuming and committees solicited input from all sectors of the citizenry. Multiple drafts were drawn up over a three-year period in which the BSPP claimed that over eight million people provided input. The final step in the process was to demilitarize the political process by having the key governmental officials resign their military posts.

Under the new structure, Burma was to become a one-party socialist state. The population was to vote on a referendum to approve the new constitution. The legislative branch would be unicameral with members elected to four-year terms. The legislature would elect the state council and eventually a chairman of the council. A key goal of the new administration was to eliminate excessive bureaucracy. In theory, more power would be in the hands of the population. The new governmental system officially started on March 2, 1974. In reality, Ne Win maintained total control of the Burmese government.

Problems engulfed the new administration from the start. Flooding during the summer of 1974 led to a cholera epidemic, which the government was unable to handle. At the same time, the regime was trying to quell economic crisis on several fronts.

The final crisis of 1974 occurred when retired UN Secretary-General U Thant died in November. Ne Win refused to grant a state funeral for possibly the most prominent international figure to emerge from Burma. Historic animosity between Win and Thant dated back to the 1950s. Over 50,000 student protesters turned out wanting Thant to receive proper burial and the honor deserving such an important world leader. The military refused to grant a state service and initially closed the universities and cut off communications with the outside world. As the protests turned violent, bloodshed ensued with over 4,000 arrests, and 74 protesters wounded and 9 killed. Martial law was declared in Rangoon for the next 18 months. Universities were closed and reopened on several occasions during this period.

In addition to student unrest, Ne Win faced growing opposition from Buddhist activists. The BSPP believed that the leaders of the Buddhist community were in collusion with the student activities during the turmoil of late 1974. The government responded by attempting to purge and purify the monastic order. The government now required that all members of the monkhood had to register with the authorities. At the same time, Ne Win attempted to gain favor by releasing 14,000 political prisoners and striving for reconciliation with former enemies, including U Nu. Numerous individuals who were involved in antigovernment activities several years earlier were allowed to return, under the condition that they stay out of politics.

The later years of the BSPP were plagued with threats to Ne Win, some real and some perceived. Multiple plots were uncovered during the late 1970s and 1980s. Several BSPP members were gaining in popularity at the expense of the longtime leader. A party vote taken in the late 1970s showed greater support for San Yu. Because of this unfavorable vote 113 party members were purged out of the party. The overall opinion was that the regime had become corrupt and was out of touch with the population. Under growing pressure, Ne Win resigned as president, but remained in control over the party. Over the next several years, multiple purges occurred, including a massive shakeup of the military hierarchy.

Ultimately a combination of political and economic unrest set the stage for the evens of 1988. Confidence in the state was at an all-time low and a legitimacy crisis loomed on the horizon. The BSPP had failed to improve the livelihoods of the Burmese citizenry. Any threats from insurgent elements had dissipated as well as external support for any groups opposing the regime. The only group within Burma that saw any improvement in living conditions was the military hierarchy, whose control remained unquestioned by the late 1980s.

11

Revolutionary Upheaval and Aborted Democracy, 1988–1990

The most tragic period in modern Burmese history occurred during a time span of 26 months in 1988–1990. In this rather brief period, the hopes and dreams for the modernization and democratization of Burma were brutally crushed by the repressive military junta that controlled the country at the time. A people's revolution was underway that promised to usher in a new and bright future for the citizens of this impoverished Southeast Asian state. Initially the "year of rage" was to usher in a new era for Burma. Elections, which promised to lead to a new governing structure for Burma, were held, but the resulting change never transpired. Instead Burma became an Orwellian nightmare of pain, suffering, and repression.

THE SPARK: TEASHOP UPHEAVAL

Disillusionment against the regime increased with the decision in September 1987 to demonetize 25, 35, and 75 kyat notes. Speculation abounds about the rational for the decision, but astrological advice probably played a significant role. Protests quickly ensued as a significant portion of the population saw their savings disappear in a few short days. Universities were sporadically closed over the coming months.

On March 12, 1988, students from the Rangoon Institute of Technology (RIT) clashed with local youths at Sanda Win teashop near the campus in the northern part of the city. The actual violence started over the music being played in the teashop. One of the customers hit a student over the head with a stool. The police were called in, but one of the key architects of the violence was released because his father was a politically connected local official of the Burma Socialist Program Party (BSPP). Outraged students marched to the local party office, causing damage to furniture and smashing windows. In the ensuing brawl, one student protestor was stabbed. Several hundred students gathered and marched to the teashop location where the initial trouble originated. Soldiers and police raided the RIT campus, escalating the already high level of tension.

Put into the context of worsening economic conditions, this protest and response initiated the most significant upheaval in Burma in the independence period. A key military leader, Sein Lwin, head of the notorious Lon Htein (riot police), acted in an overly aggressive fashion, which heightened tensions. Once the protesters arrived at the teashop, the Lon Htein attacked them with hoses, clubs, teargas, and firearms. A student by the name of Maung Phone Maw was killed in the clash. Over the next two days, protests increased as students from Rangoon Arts and Sciences University (RASU) and other local schools collaborated on staging rallies and protests. The movement was demanding the resignation of Ne Win along with steps toward multiparty democracy.

On March 16, the students marched to the now infamous White Bridge, an embankment along the western shore of Inya Lake between RIT and the RASU. The Lon Htein blocked the students. Scores were killed and many were beaten to death and several drowned in the lake. Women were sexually abused in a carnage that lasted approximately one hour. The authorities quickly disposed of the bodies and attempted to clean the area of the bloody mess. The following day, more arrests occurred at the RASU campus, as protesters demanded the government conduct an inquiry into the violence in recent days. The police arrested over 1,000 students, sending them to the infamous Insein jail. On Bloody Friday, March 18, students as well as ordinary citizens marched and rioted in route to the Sule pagoda in central Rangoon. So many arrests occurred that police had to ship detainees off to jails away from the capital. In one especially horrific incident, 41 students suffocated while being held in a police paddy wagon. The vehicle was parked for several hours in route to a jail transfer. The authorities closed the universities, sending students home and leading to the subsiding of the upheaval. Ultimately, the protesters lacked leadership and a coherent strategy. Calm returned to the capital as Ne Win departed for his usual vacation trip to Europe.

The subsequent investigation was an attempt by the authorities to conceal the facts of the incidents. The report's findings were published in *Working*

People's Daily in mid May. The number of casualties was grossly underscored. The type of ammunition used by the security forces was covered up (the claim that automatic weapons were not used proved to be false). Finally, the police claimed that outside agitators caused much of the disruption.

Protests continued into the summer with some estimates stating that over one million people in Rangoon took part at some point in time. Than Shwe, the deputy chief of staff, was mortified and secured his family in a compound with additional security forces present. Adding more fuel to the fire, rumors throughout the country stated the United States had moved naval ships into the waters off the coast. Fear of a possible international invasion gained momentum. In reality, this was totally untrue and Western nations never made any sort of movement toward Myanmar or ever contemplated such a policy shift.

Criticism of the regime continued to mount. Retired Brigadier General Aung Gyi released a scathing indictment of the handling of the situation. Gyi had also criticized Ne Win's failed economic policies. The general encouraged Ne Win to distance himself from the military hardliners who were responsible for the mishandling of the protests. With such a long-time regime supporter abandoning the regime and openly criticizing policy, it was becoming apparent that change was in the air.

SUMMER OF HOPE: 1988

Protests reignited in Burma following the opening of the universities in late May. By late June, student's demands included the rebuilding of the Rangoon Student Union, as well as more autonomy within the educational bureaucracy. The regime once again closed down the RASU. Protests persisted as the government sent in the Lon Htein to quell the disturbances. The students fended off the riot police by fleeing into alley and backstreet market areas. Protesters fought back and inflicted casualties not seen during the White Bridge massacre in March. Twenty officers were killed in the melee.

The government imposed long-term curfews and banned public gatherings. Food distribution was difficult, as vendors could not get to the markets. Riots and disorder was spreading to other cities as Burma was quickly approaching chaos. One ploy of the regime was to blame the Muslim minority population for the unrest. The regime assumed that the religious antagonism would take pressure off of the government. This had been a tactic used by the government on a few occasions since 1962. This time it did not work since the problems were much more severe and widespread.

By July, the regime called a party congress to deal with the situation. Ne Win's speech to the congress asked for a national referendum on a multiparty system. Second, Ne Win also asked to be able to resign from his government post. He stated that further bloodshed needed to be avoided and civil disturbances must come to an end. A final point in the speech claimed that General Aung Gyi bore the responsibility for the destruction of the Rangoon Student Union Building in 1962, a point that Ne Win seemed to be obsessed with.

The focus of the government turned to economic reform. Aye Ko proposed liberalization of trade, banking reform, and joint public-private ventures. It was obvious that the early socialist policies were dead. The delegates at the party meeting accepted the resignation of Ne Win, but rejected the referendum idea concerning a multiparty system. Several scholars speculate that the accepting of the retirement of Ne Win and rejection of the referendum that was requested by other long-time party leaders Aye Ko, Sein Lwin, Kyaw Htin, and Tun Tin, was simply a ploy to keep the decision making in the hands of the old guard.

The movement picked up momentum by July. Protesters included the working class and most of the urban populations within Burma. The vital element that was missing was the military. It seemed as if a split in the tatmadaw was eminent. Facilitating a split in the military would, in the minds of many, lead to the ultimate fall of the regime. The regime used ethnic minority troops, many from the Kachin group, to suppress the protesters in the cities. One incident in particular showed the extent that the tatmadaw was willing to go in order to stay in power. On August 10, troops entered Rangoon General Hospital and opened fire on wounded protesters. Eventually the troops turned their weapons on hospital staff and innocent bystanders. This was a point of no return. The population could no longer trust the military, which some had viewed as a protector of the state. The honor and prestige of the military was lost forever.

By mid August opposition was growing. Noncommunist groups were calling for an alliance with the student organizations. Several thousand students fled to the Thailand border to join with the insurgents. Unfortunately, fighting between insurgency factions broke out, making the development of a coherent strategy impossible. Second, the All-Burma Bar Council fell in line with the students, demanding an end to martial law and an opening of civil society in Burma. Most importantly, Aung San Suu Kyi sent a letter to the government asking for sincere mediation efforts between the state and the protesters.

Sein Lwin resigned the chairmanship of the BSPP in early August. Protesters clamored for his arrest, blaming him for the killings of March and May. Lwin who was known as "the butcher of Rangoon," probably fled overseas. The student movement seemed to have won a major victory. The death toll at this point was over 3,000. The regime continued a policy of cover-up and denial. Martial law remained in place. The regime was weakening and at the party congress it was announced that a civilian, Dr. Maung Maung, was taking over the leadership helm. Maung, the attorney general at the time, would be the first civilian leader in Burma's history.

During August, several urban areas including Rangoon came under the control of the protesters. The antigovernment opposition now included a sizeable number of workers as well as a growing number of monks. Maung Maung was considered an unacceptable replacement leader. Maung was thought of as a puppet of former leader Ne Win. The opposition wanted Maung to resign by September 7. Concessions followed with the releasing of prominent leaders such as Aung Gyi as well as the lifting of martial law. Finally, Maung promised a second BSPP congress to decide on a referendum for free and fair elections. To help guide the process, the BSPP formed an election commission to oversee the transition.

During this tension-filled month, the tatmadaw remained mostly out of sight. The state continued to decline with the economy in a free fall and public facilities nonfunctioning and strikes commonplace. The population enjoyed a greater degree of freedom than anytime in Burmese history as civil liberties emerged, including a free press. Several opposition leaders openly emerged to challenge the legitimacy of the state. Aung Gyi gained a following, as well as former prime minister U Nu who claimed that the entire governing structure from 1962 to 1988 was illegal.

Law and order partially broke down because of the government's continued attempts to foster the chaos. Jails were empted, and looting and destruction was permitted by the military. Ultimately, these actions or inactions of September 1988 were a planned and coordinated effort to sow chaos so that the military could return to power. The regime formed an antistrike committee to discuss potential assassinations, dates for a coup d'état, and possible terrorists acts to facilitate the military's return.

The military continued to lay the groundwork for a potential coup. General Saw Maung stated that the people lived in fear and that they longed for peace and stability to return to Burma. The military also blamed the unrest of foreign elements that had infiltrated Burmese society. The tatmadaw claimed to be the defender of the Burmese nation.

Student leaders and protesters were unable to seize the moment. Intense factionalizations as well as a lack of coordination lessened the change for success. On September 12, the most significant threat to the regime emerged with the formation of the National League for Democracy (NLD). This coalition included the three most prominent opposition leaders, with Aung Gyi serving as party chairman, Tin U as vice chairman, and Aung San Suu Kyi as general secretary. The NLD wanted a formation of an interim government that would transition to a true democratic system.

THE ROLE OF AUNG SAN SUU KYI

The most prominent pro-democracy leader to emerge was Aung San Suu Kyi, daughter of the legendary founder of Burma, General Aung San. After high school Suu Kyi attended Lady Sri Ram College in Delhi, where she had moved with her mother in 1960. Her mother would be the ambassador to India from 1960 to 1967. Suu Kyi spent one year at Sri Ram College prior to gaining admission to St. Hugh's College, Oxford. She was one of the first Burmese to gain acceptance there.

By all accounts, Suu Kyi was a serious student, proud of her Burmese heritage. She for the most part rejected the decadent lifestyle of 1960s university life. Suu Kyi majored in politics, philosophy, and economics. Ironically, while studying abroad in Great Britain, Burmese democracy was collapsing at home. Interestingly, Suu Kyi avoided politics for the most part. She did not speak out about the Vietnam War or become involved in any way with campus protests or demonstrations. She also did not socialize very much with the Burmese community in or around the campus. Aung San Suu Kyi graduated from Oxford with honors in 1967.

Aung San Suu Kyi was uncertain about her career path and direction. She ultimately moved to New York City in 1969. Suu Kyi took a job with the United Nations working for the Advisory Committee on Administrative and Budgetary Questions. She simultaneously worked on an English Literature degree at New York University. Suu Kyi shared an apartment with Ma Than E, a family friend. This was an advantageous time to work at the United Nations since the Secretary-General U Thant was Burmese. Suu Kyi stayed at the organization for three years.

While at the United Nations, Suu Kyi kept in contact with future Tibetan scholar Michael Aris whom she had known during their time together at Oxford University. After a long period of correspondence, she visited him in Bhutan in 1970. She returned to New York engaged. They married in 1972 and Suu Kyi subsequently left her job in New York at the UN to join Michael. His studies took the couple from Bhutan back to Oxford for several years. During this time, the couple had two children: Alex in 1973 and Kim in 1977.

Aung San Suu Kyi published several academic essays and in 1984 she authored a brief biography of her late father. In 1985, Aung San Suu Kyi won a scholarship to study at the University of Kyoto in Japan. The family eventually moved to India where Michael was a visiting fellow at the Indian Institute for Advanced Studies. Suu Kyi was about to begin graduate work on Burmese literature at London University's School of Oriental and Asian Studies when she was called back home to Burma to deal with her ailing mother who had suffered a stroke. Upon her arrival, she never became involved nor made public statements regarding the politics in Burma.

When Suu Kyi arrived in Burma, General Ne Win had been in power for 26 years. The country was spiraling downward both economically and socially. As time progressed, Suu Kyi continued to see firsthand the suffering the Burmese population at the hands of the brutal dictatorship. At first, Suu Kyi offered to play the role of mediator between the government and students. Initially, she did not want any sort of leadership role in the ongoing rebellion.

Circumstances changed during the turbulent year of 1988. Suu Kyi's first public appearance was at the Shwedagon pagoda on August 26, 1988. According to Peter Popham's biography of Suu Kyi, *The Lady and the Peacock,* over half a million people showed up for her speech. In answering her critics, Aung San Suu Kyi stated, "It is true that I have lived abroad. It is also true that I am married to a foreigner. These facts have never interfered and will never interfere with or lessen my love and devotion for my country by any measure or degree. Another thing which people have been saying is that I know nothing of Burmese politics. The trouble is that I know too much." (56). She called the struggle of 1988 the second struggle for national independence. Suu Kyi also called on the military to become a force that the people can place trust in, something that her father had always strived for.

The election commission met with the key NLD leaders to discuss the formation of the system. The major concern was that the current party in control, the BSPP, would have an unfair advantage by already being entrenched within Burmese society. Furthermore, the manpower and financial advantages of the BSPP were obvious. The NLD decided to hold a national assembly in Rangoon to support the formation of an interim government, abolishment of the BSPP, and the disbanding of the election commission. The political crisis in Burma had reached critical mass.

On Sunday September 18, the military staged a coup establishing the State Law and Order Restoration Council (SLORC). The tatmadaw had become worried that members of the armed forces were starting to defect to the pro-democracy movement. The 1986 People's Power movement in the Philippines may have influenced the regime's actions at this time. The Marcos regime had been deposed mostly because of the decision by the military to side with the opposition. The day before the coup, the military issued a statement saying that the main duties of the armed forces remained: work for national unity, perpetuation of the state, and work for the consolidation and strengthening of sovereignty. In the end, overwhelming loyalty to the military remained in place.

General Saw Maung was the chairman of SLORC. The essential platform of the regime was: restoration of law, order, peace and tranquility; providing security; assist the population regarding food, clothing, and shelter; and the eventual fulfillment of multiparty elections. The Pyithu Hluttaw and council of ministers were quickly abolished. The previous constitution was no longer relevant. The junta would include 19 high-ranking members of the military. The key subordinates to Saw Maung included Than Shwe (deputy chief of staff) and Khin Nyunt (director of defense services intelligence). It was clear that all 19 members of SLORC were Ne Win loyalists. It was apparent to all unbiased observers that the event of September 18 was a phony coup staged to reestablish clear military control in Burma.

Resistance to the military takeover was quickly destroyed. The tatmadaw was very organized and efficiently brutal. Opposition leaders were arrested and the military fired on pagodas and homes of suspected sympathizers. Strike centers and the free media were closed down. Curfews were imposed and public gatherings outlawed. Any bureaucrats who had been involved in pro-democracy organizations were fired and many were arrested. In order to conceal their real intentions, the tatmadaw claimed that the coup was a "temporary mandate" that would end following the elections.

TIGHTENING THE NOOSE: SLORC IN POWER

Burmese civil society was brutality crushed by SLORC in the late summer of 1989. However, it became apparent quickly that SLORC planned on keeping the schedule for multiparty elections. The election commission remained in place, as the regime believed that by holding the elections, legitimacy would be gained. Second, Burma was in desperate need of foreign assistance. It quickly became apparent to the regime that Aung San Suu Kyi's popularity and prestige, especially with powerful Western powers, was going to challenge the junta's claim to govern.

On November 8, the government press agency announced that the elections would be held on May 27, 1990. The regime would monitor all electoral activities including rallies, media, and publications. By February, over 2,300 candidates had filled to run from approximately 480 parties. SLORC made it clear that it would remain in power in the postelection transition period while a new constitution was drafted.

There was still a sense of uncertainty regarding whether the 1947 or 1974 constitution was legitimate. It seemed that SLORC assumed that power would be transferred to the Pyithu Hluttaw (people's assembly) at the appropriate time. The assembly was considered to be the most significant branch of government. A troubling concern was over the meaning of the election process. The junta believed that the purpose of the process was to strengthen the regime, while the opposition believed the election to be an exercise in popular sovereignty. This debate over the true meaning of the process haunted modern Burma for the foreseeable future.

The NLD was the most significant opposition movement in Burma. Faction-alism would damage the party in late 1988, as Aung Gyi decided to abandon the movement. The retired general claimed that communists had infiltrated the NLD. The NLD had adapted the fighting peacock as the symbol of the movement, something that the early student movement had used as a symbol. The electoral commission forbid the use of religious symbols as well as ani-mals for party logos, so the NLD selected the bamboo peasant hat to represent the people of Burma.

In December 1988, Aung San Suu Kyi's mother passed away. Over 100,000 cit-izens, including key members of SLORC and a large contingent of foreign ambassadors, attended her state funeral. Suu Kyi embarked on a massive tour across the nation in 1989. She spoke on the theme of national unity in the ethnically diverse regions of the countries. The regime's tactics against her included harassment, intimidation, and the false imprisonment of NLD members. On an ominous day in April, several members of a military con-tingency drew their rifles on Suu Kyi. A last-minute order to desist by a captain probably saved her life. This highlighted the potential problem of safety on the campaign trail. Suu Kyi continued to stress nonviolence to her followers. As anniversaries of the key dates from the "year of rage" ap-proached, tensions increased. The military prepared for potential confronta-tions by literally changing the physical landscape of key areas. Trees were cut down, walls were built, and the relocation of urban resistances was un-dertaken. Up to 500,000 residents would be impacted by SLORC's relocation policies.

Additionally, SLORC intensified a smear campaign against Aung San Suu Kyi. The focus of the attack was centered on her time away from Burma as well as her British husband, Michael Aris, and her supposed ties to elements of the communist party. Furthermore, the regime claimed that Suu Kyi was tainted by Western values. These tactics proved counterproductive as Suu Kyi's popularity continued to rise. A worried military decided to place both Aung San Suu Kyi and Tin U under house arrest.

In the summer of 1989, in order to add credibility to the communist ac-cusation, the tatmadaw released "Burma Communist Party's Conspiracy to Take over State Power." This lengthy document accused the leadership of the NLD of being in collusion with the communists. To further the conspiracy charges, the Ministry of Information issued an additional 300-page manu-script detailing major enemies of the state. Included in this work was rightist factions, journalists, foreign diplomats, U.S. Congressional members, minor-ity populations, especially the Karens, and of course the key NLD leaders Suu Kyi and Tin U. These massive conspiracy theories were for the most part ignored by the general population.

Concern emerged over a potential split in the tatmadaw as Suu Kyi's cred-itability increased. The regime continued with an aggressive public relations campaign centered on discounting the atrocities of 1988 along with the es-sential role played by the tatmadaw in keeping Burma safe and secure. The underlying culprit working against Burma was foreign elements. Western media and human rights organizations constituted a new form of colonial-ism. This xenophobia has plagued the leadership of Burma for most of its history.

THE ELECTIONS OF 1990: TRIUMPH AND TRAGEDY IN MODERN BURMA

In early 1990, the two top leaders of the NLD Aung San Suu Kyi and Tin U were both disqualified from running for office. With literally thousands of party members incarcerated by early 1990, a discussion ensued within the NLD as to whether to boycott the elections. The regime made it clear that outside monitoring would not be allowed. The creditability of the process was in serious doubt. Ultimately, the NLD decided to continue to participate and would run candidates for 451 of the 492 assembly seats.

Surprisingly, the SLORC went to great lengths to ensure the electoral proc-ess was credible. Ballots would be secret and standards were set to guarantee accuracy. Provisions for absentee ballots were set and procedural mechanics were in place to establish transparency. Martial law was revoked in the period prior to Election Day. Finally, the military kept a low profile while the election took place.

The results were a shock to SLORC. The NLD won nearly 60 percent of the vote and 392 of 485 constituencies contested. The pro-government National Unity Party garnered 21 percent and only 10 seats. The voter turnout was the largest for any election in the history of Burma with 72.6 percent turning out to participate. It was painfully obvious that SLORC's plan had gone terribly wrong. Some evidence points to the fact that members of the tatmadaw and their families may have indeed supported the NLD candidates. The regime's paranoia increased.

The NLD thanked the regime for carrying out a free and fair electoral proc-ess. However, after several weeks, apprehension set in as SLORC did not take any steps to seat the new Pyithu Hluttaw. The regime was not sure what ac-tion to take. The party line was that the tatmadaw would continue to fulfill its promise to maintain law and order and work toward the goal of providing the basic necessities for the citizens of Burma. Until these goals were met, a transition could not take place. Furthermore, the junta focused on the need to put forth a new constitution prior to any transition taking place. This seemed not only illogical, but also an obvious stall tactic.

SLORC formalized its noncompliance with Declaration 1/90 issued on July 27, which stated the following: transfer of power could not take place until a new constitution was finalized; representatives were elected to draft a constitution; and until a new constitution was in place, SLORC would maintain total authority for governing Burma. The document made it clear that all legislative, executive, and judicial powers rested with SLORC.

The response from the NLD came in the form of the Gandhi Hall Declaration issued several days after the SLORC announcement. The Gandhi Hall Declaration called for the convening of the Pyithu Hluttaw as soon as possible, with a September deadline set. This was the expectation of the people. The declaration also called on SLORC to enter into negotiations with the NLD to bring about reconciliation. Furthermore, the immediate release of key NLD leaders and other political prisoners was essential. The NLD also claimed that the model for a new constitution would be the 1947 document rather than the previous constitution of 1974.

The sangha attempted to take action to help facilitate change. Monks joined with NLD supporters to commemorate the events of August 1988 often referred to as 8888. To pressure the military, monks were told not to accept offerings from the tatmadaw. This turning over of the offering bowl is the equivalent of excommunication. Offerings are the main way Buddhists earn merit. Since most members of the military were Buddhist, this tactic could have potentially damaged the legitimacy of the regime. The leadership retaliated by arresting monks, raiding monasteries, and pressuring the Buddhist leadership to resend earlier orders. By late October, the government took indirect control over the monks.

International pressure on SLORC increased during the summer of 1990. Rather than reconciliation, the junta responded with internal repression. Hundreds were arrested and pressure mounted on the remaining NLD members to force Suu Kyi and Tin U out of the party. The entire election process helped to flush out additional opponents of the regime. This in turn helped the junta to further consolidate power.

12

Continued Dictatorship and Lost Hope, 1990–2007

Following the electoral fiasco of 1990, the main goal of the military was to maintain the status quo and, as quickly as possible, remove the National League for Democracy (NLD) and their marquee leader out of the public spotlight. Over the next two decades, the government would engage in a constant battle in an attempt to maintain a façade of legitimacy based on the obligation of maintaining law and order with the intention of suppressing the rightfully elected leaders of the country. This battle would spill over into nearly every aspect of the public and private realm. The economic, social, cultural, and international policies of Myanmar would be impacted by this never-ending contest.

SLORC TIGHTENS GRIP

One interesting decision made by the regime in the pre-election period was to announce the name change to the country, towns, and population. In mid October 1988, the ruling State Law and Order Restoration Council (SLORC) enacted the "Law on the Substitution of Terms." The "Socialist Republic of the Union of Burma" was changed to "Union of Burma" as well as additional titles and terms. During May and June of 1989, SLORC went a step further and decided to change the name of the country to the Union of Myanmar. The rationale was that the name Burma carried with it colonial connotations and by going back to what SLORC thought was the original "proper" pronunciation, "Myanmar," the vestiges of colonial would be removed.

SLORC remained vague concerning the future political situation in Myanmar. By 1992, meetings were held with the representatives of the parties that were not decertified for the purpose of establishing a constitutional convention. The first convention consisted of 702 delegates of which only 14 percent won seats in the May 1990 elections. The constitutional drafting process was delayed and a clear timetable seemed to be a low priority. The process moved forward at an extremely slow pace and many participants felt that the entire effort was not taken seriously. Many observers speculate that the rationale behind the gradual movement was to wear down the opposition so that the tatmadaw could consolidate control.

The basic principles emphasized by the national convention in September 1993 included the clear establishment of a union system with seven regions and seven states. Furthermore, self-administered regions were established for national races. Multiparty democracy with a president that would serve as both head of state and head of government would be instituted. A bicameral legislature, supreme court, and clear separation of powers would be implemented. Finally, a free-market economic system with a nonaligned foreign policy would be emphasized.

The role of the military in the new governmental system was the most significant element, however. Twenty-five percent of the legislative seats were reserved for the military. The tatmadaw would also have significant influence in the selection of the president and the government would have no control over military decision making. Even with these obvious pro-military decrees being passed, it was clear that a new government would not be established for a considerable period of time.

The military control was put in a bit of turmoil in 1992. Saw Maung conducted a purge of the government with nearly 15,000 civil servants losing their positions. He was to serve for 18 months with Than Shwe as his deputy. Diplomats that met Than Shwe recall him as being very quiet while attending meetings. He was difficult to read and it was impossible to discern whether he agreed with the decisions being implemented by Saw Maung.

It was also apparent that Saw Maung's health, both physically and mentally, was in sharp decline. Several accounts from diplomats inside and outside of Myanmar claim that Saw Maung was "more than a little deranged." His erratic and unstable behavior concerned fellow members of the military establishment. Concrete examples of his mental decline occurred on several outings during 1992. Some speculate that at some point Saw Maung suffered a nervous breakdown. He had threatened to shoot several of his generals during a golf outing and repeatedly made claims to be the early Burmese King Kyanzittha. This later claim was repeated in a speech broadcast on television. In that same broadcast, he denied being a practitioner of black magic and claimed that martial law equaled no law at all. In addition, Saw Maung also struggled with diabetes and alcoholism. Maung became violent at times and during several fits of rage he was known to throw furniture and actually injured himself during one particular bout. At one press conference, the leader ranted and raved about the differences between Christianity and Buddhism. His embarrassing behavior led journalist John Casey to claim that Saw Maung was a buffoon. Some pundits speculate that the awarding of the Nobel Peace Prize to Aung San Suu Kyi may have helped to push Saw Maung over the edge. Rumors were circulating early in his reign that several keys generals were planning on replacing the unstable leader. Within Myanmar, one rumor circulated that fellow generals Khin Nyunt and Than Shwe had drugged Saw Maung. Another version of the events leading up to Saw Maung's demise proposes that Nyunt and Shwe collaborated together to bring down Saw Maung. Military intelligence agents contacted regional commanders to inform them of the proposed replacement of Saw Maung based on his irrational behavior. Informed of the decision to replace him, Saw Maung quietly went into retirement in March 1992. His official resignation cited health reasons.

A supposed power struggle emerged between Khin Nyunt, a close confidant of Ne Win, who held the position of head of military intelligence, and Than Shwe, who had already positioned himself in line behind Saw Maung. In April, General Than Shwe emerged victorious in a leadership struggle over Khin Nyunt. Speculation abounds that Nyunt encouraged Than Shwe to take the top spot in the belief that he would not last long. This view was widely circulated as many visiting diplomats speculated that Than Shwe would be a short-term leader. Khin Nyunt believed that he could overtake Shwe easily in due course. Than Shwe was considered less ambitious, more conservative, and less of a threat to the military establishment. Many within the ranks of the military were shocked at his takeover because he was not considered to have the intellect to hold the position. Than Shwe, it seemed, wanted to be underestimated by his contemporaries and potential foes. In this vein, he could come across as unambitious and parochial, but in reality he turned into a savvy and ruthless dictator. Than Shwe was officially sworn in as SLORC chairman on April 23, 1992.

Than Shwe's early career actually mirrors that of Ne Win. They both started in governmental positions as postal clerks and later both were involved in the psychological-warfare component of the tatmadaw. Once he assumed power, Shwe began holding secret late-night cabinet meetings with key members of the tatmadaw who would eventually become his key loyalists. Future leader Thein Sein would be included in this late-night leadership faction. On several occasions, Than Shwe informally called on Ne Win to get his approval for projects that were being undertaken. Though he did not in any way have a power base that could threaten Shwe, it was considered respectful to consult with him and probably help to establish his creditability and legitimacy within the ranks of the military. Ne Win gave his blessings to the direction in which Than Shwe was taking Myanmar.

As Than Shwe assumed the position of head of the army, defense chief, head of SLORC, and prime minister, his power was unmatched. Considered a drab and uninspiring figure, Than Shwe was firm and more of a hardliner on policy than his predecessor. Later, Shwe would purge Nyunt, who was eventually charged with insubordination, corruption, and dereliction of duty. Many of his associates within the military intelligence organization were imprisoned, while Nyunt was allowed to retire because of ill health. This event was the culmination of a power struggle between the military and intelligence agencies. In the end, the entire military intelligence operation was abolished with Shwe claiming this to be a major step in cleaning up corruption and mismanagement within the state of Myanmar.

The NLD attempted to negotiate in a constructive manner with Than Shwe. The refusal to transfer power to the rightfully elected government was the main point of contention. Furthermore, the NLD and Chairman Aung Shwe felt that the regime continually stonewalled the movement and delayed any substantive meetings regarding the democratic transition process. These tactics delayed the formation of a national parliament in line with the election results of 1990. Genuine negotiations in reality were never held. The strategy was of course to show the futility in supporting the NLD. In order to promote the façade of having an inclusionary policy, Than Shwe invited approximately 80 members of the NLD to participate in the national convention process. It was obvious that the Shwe's goal was to monopolize the decision-making process within the convention. The majority of delegates were either military associates of the dictator or members of the business community, which had strong ties to the military apparatus. The NLD protested the rigged process and boycotted the convention. Ultimately, the NLD had little or no input into the framing of the constitution.

Than Shwe's main goals included convening the national convention in order to begin the process of constructing a constitution. In addition, major policy initiatives included state restructuring, centralization of the military structure, educational modifications, and a declaration of a ceasefire with the Karens. Tension remained between the tatmadaw and military intelligence. Part of this factionalism had to do with the competing personalities of Shwe and Khin Nyunt, who dually played a role in the demise of Saw Maung. Than Shwe selected Maung Aye from the Eastern Region Command to serve as his new military chief. A more direct challenge to Khin Nyunt came from the fact that Shwe did not appoint him vice chairman of party. This move made it clear to everyone following the process that a rivalry was underway. As a way to cloak his conservative agenda, Than Shwe made initial policy steps in order to be perceived as more of a moderate. For example, political prisoners were released and international organizations such as the International Red Cross and Amnesty International were once again allowed to return to Myanmar. Possibly the most promising sign was Shwe's initial crackdown against corruption within the government.

These early moves may have been implemented to help Than Shwe consolidate power. Nyunt may have had more support in the cabinet. This rift at times spilled over into policy debates. On issues ranging from the speed and intent of the national convention to how to effectively deal with the NLD and Aung San Suu Kyi, to issues of foreign policy, this spilt within the government had significant ramifications.

WHAT'S IN A NAME: FROM SLORC TO SPDC

SLORC decided that in order to reconfigure the regime's image, a name change was necessary. The government had employed two public-relations companies to help the regime soften its persona. Jackson Bash and Jefferson Waterman International were paid exorbitant sums to polish the regime's image. The State Law and Order Protection Council officially became the State Peace and Development Council (SPDC) in 1997. A reshuffling within the power structure occurred with only the top four generals remaining in their current positions. During this same year, the regime gained admittance into the Association of Southeast Asian Nations (ASEAN). Some regional experts believe the name change was done in part to help secure the ASEAN admission. It was also believed that this surface-level softening could enhance the tourism industry. The name change did not lead to any significant policy movement from the junta. This may have been a missed opportunity for Myanmar to open up internationally. For the junta, democracy was still in a long transitional phase, for which the generals would set the agenda and timeline.

THE NEVER-ENDING INSURGENCY PROBLEM

The junta had reasons to be worried. They faced internal opposition from the NLD and supporters (both domestically and internationally) of Aung San Suu Kyi, as well as the never-ending ethnic-based insurgencies. The tactics employed by the government would be to eradicate the insurgency problem by making separate ceasefire agreements with the different movements—a kind of divide-and-conquer strategy. Giving the key leaders either a certain level of autonomy or some sort financial incentive would help the regime achieve its goal.

Many student protesters from the initial pro-democracy movement had fled to the border areas to join in an alliance with the ethnic fighters opposing the government. It is estimated that between 8,000 and 10,000 persons fled the urban centers to join with the insurgency fighters. This coalition would be known as the Democratic Alliance of Burma (DAB). This was a noteworthy achievement because virtually every government since independence had demonized the ethnic populations as criminals and savages never to be trusted. SLORC's repressive policies had brought this unusual alliance together.

The coalition ran into numerous problems from the onset. Expectations were high that international assistance would be forthcoming. The condemnation of the electoral scam and the amount of global coverage of the pro-democracy efforts led the student leaders to believe that aid and military assistance would easily be secured. This assistance never materialized in any significant way. The students who headed to the border areas were not accustomed to the very difficult living conditions in the jungle and mountain regions. The harsh conditions led to widespread disease, especially malaria. Furthermore, the student organizations were beset with extreme factionalism. This problem plagued the pro-democracy movement dating back to its origins in 1988.

The insurgents also found it difficult to work with the new arrivals. The student resistance members were neither used to the harsh conditions nor were they trained to fight. They quickly became a liability. Within a few months, many students took an offer of amnesty from the tatmadaw and returned to their home provinces. Unfortunately, many were imprisoned after surrendering to the authorities. Others fled to Thailand and eventually migrated to the West, settling in the United States, Canada, and Western Europe. This subsequently led to a brain drain in which many of the best and brightest young men and women from Myanmar fled abroad because of the lack of opportunity in their home country.

The DAB included nearly 20 organizations. Only two major groups, the Communist Party of Burma and the Mong Tai Army (Shan state), remained out of the coalition. The ultimate goal was to have a true federalist system for Myanmar. Unfortunately, most groups within the coalition remained on the periphery of society, unable to make any sort of inroads within the main population centers in Myanmar. The government also started offering concessions to numerous ethnic insurgents. Rebels who signed ceasefire agreements in many cases would be permitted to keep their weapons. By granting more autonomy to local groups, SLORC bought time to take care of more serious insurgent threats to the regime.

Insurgents were permitted to maintain cross-border trade in everything from timber to precious gems. A growing dark side of the trade included an expansion of opium production and distribution to the thriving sex-trade in which young Burmese girls would be sold into slavery in Thailand and elsewhere. A significant blow to the antigovernment insurgents was the implosion of the Burmese Communist Party (BCP). As global communism was waning, the communist party no longer received backing from China. More and more of the resources needed to stay afloat came from the growing opium trade. SLORC's goal was to divide and rule the insurgents by making a pact with remnants of the BCP. By doing this, the tatmadaw was able to turn more of its attention and military might against the ethnic insurgents within the DAB. A final initiative that helped the tatmadaw was a forced relocation or ethnic cleansing policy implemented by the regime. The relocation policy convinced many ethnic groups to cut a deal with the government.

The cornerstone of the eradication efforts by the tatmadaw was the "four cuts" strategy. The regime attempted to cut food, funds, intelligence, and recruits from insurgent strongholds. During the peak of the four-cuts operation, over 2,500 villages were destroyed with over one million peasants being displaced. The rationale behind this brutal campaign was to make the insurgents deal with the government and lay down their arms.

Ultimately, the longest running and most threatening insurgency organization continued to be the Karen National Union (KNU). As a result of the divide-and-conquer strategy, the military was able to concentrate more troops against the Karens by 1994. After decades of holding its own against the military, the movement was devastated in December 1994, when a Buddhist Karen faction formed a separate organization called the Democratic Karen Buddhist Army (DKBA). The DKBA gave the tatmadaw vital intelligence information on the KNU, leading to the fall of the Karen stronghold of Manerplaw in late January 1995. The Karen insurgency maintains a thin presence in Myanmar, having little or no effect on government policy.

Tension still exists in border areas that continue to be out of the reach of the tatmadaw. Attempts to integrate ethnic insurgent forces into regular tatmadaw units are difficult. The loss of autonomy on the part of multiple groups including the Kachin will continue to plague the junta. As recently as September 2009, refugee influx from Kachin province into China created regional chaos as thousands of peasants fled across the border in search of sanctuary. This actually caused a temporary rift between the Myanmar and Chinese governments.

SOCIAL ILLS IN CONTEMPORARY MYANMAR

A significant side effect of the change in insurgency dynamics in the early 1990s was the proliferation of the drug economy in Myanmar and surrounding areas. Initially, the drug trade enhanced the BCP's status by helping to fund the movement during the 1980s. Later, as the problem of drug abuse plagued China, pressure was applied on the BCP to curtail drug production. This rift between China and the BCP eventually led to the demise of the movement. This change in China's policy coincided with an opening of significant cross border trade relations with SLORC.

Ultimately, the end of the ethnic insurgency problem exacerbated the overall drug situation. Drug lord Khun Sa surrendered to tatmadaw forces in 1996, easing border tension. Drug production increased significantly in the mid to late 1990s. New trafficking routes opened, as well as refiners. Between 1986 and 1996, production of opium in Myanmar doubled, impacting the availability in the United States, China, India, and Thailand. Myanmar currently accounts for 80 percent of all heroin produced in Southeast Asia. By the late 1990s, Myanmar also became a center of methamphetamine production. Overall drug use and addiction in Myanmar has increased dramatically during this period of military rule.

An additional social problem to plague Myanmar is HIV/AIDS. The increased use of drugs along with changing sexual habits and the lack of availability of condoms has compounded the crisis. The difficult task of getting reliable information from the regime makes the accuracy of data questionable. Using sources from the military, the number of infected citizens was 400,000 by the late 1990s. This makes Myanmar one of the hardest-hit countries in all of Asia. The crisis only worsens because of the regime's inability or indifference to the suffering of the population. The junta stays in denial and refuses any assistance from outside health agencies.

The proliferation of the sex trade has also played into the social demise of Myanmar. The only attempt to deal with the issue of sex trafficking was for the regime to issue general statements about morality and the evils of foreign influence of traditional culture. The dark reality is that an underground sex trade operation has been underway for the past 15 years.

ECONOMIC POLICY DURING THE SLORC/SPDC

The initial economic policy change in Myanmar was to abolish the socialist policies of the past 26 years. The regime pinned its hope on foreign investment—reemerging as the isolationist xenophobic Ne Win was no longer in control of the government. The problem for Myanmar was that as promises of democracy and an open political system faded, so did Western assistance. By 1990, SLORC was in dire straits economically. External debt neared the 5 billion dollar mark by the postelection period. Japan had provided the lion's share of relief to the junta. Future assistance was contingent on fulfilling promises made to promote democracy and human rights that SLORC adamantly opposed.

The regime promised liberalization of trade, resumption of a market economy, and generous tax relief and exemptions to foreign companies. Exemptions covered numerous sectors, including manufacturing, tourism, and agriculture. The government passed the "Union of Burma Foreign Investment Law," which guaranteed that past mistakes such as currency devaluation and nationalization of industries would not take place. The rationale behind the law was to help Myanmar reach the goal of easing the peoples' needs for food, clothing, and shelter.

A huge economic bureaucracy developed to help facilitate the new policies. The regime established a massive holding company, Union of Myanmar Economic Holdings, which was mostly owned by the Ministry of Defense and high-ranking officers. A foreign investment commission was established to help with insurance, currency matters, and regulation of the economy. The first countries to invest heavily in Myanmar were some of the neighboring states such as Japan, South Korea, and Taiwan. The appeal of cheap labor and what seemed to be a cooperative regime helped in the initial boost.

The majority of citizens in Myanmar were not benefitting from the economic changes. The currency devaluation issue was still a serious concern, as was high levels of inflation and the always-present black market. Printing more currency covered deficits. An underlying theme of the junta's economic policy was to ensure the military was taken care of at the expense of the population. Self-preservation was the main priority. Revenue was necessary to purchase military hardware, and new technology provided generous pay hikes to ensure troop loyalty following the upheavals of 1988–1990.

MYANMAR IN THE INTERNATIONAL REALM

Japan was one of the initial countries to break the ice with Myanmar, normalizing relations in February 1989. Joint business ventures emerged in the early 1990s between the government and nearly a dozen Japanese firms. The Japanese government wanted companies to take a cautious approach in dealing with the junta because of potential Western pressure over the horrendous human rights record and potential negative public relations that could be generated. A split in Japanese policy toward Myanmar developed. The more pro-business sector of the economy wanted an open door to Myanmar and the ability to do business without constraints. The foreign policy faction within the Japanese government wanted to use aid and economic policy to help promote democracy and more constructive human rights efforts. The Japanese government made multiple public statements of support to Aung San Suu Kyi, frustrating SLORC at times. However, much of Myanmar's debt was owed to the Japanese government, tempering the harsh rhetoric against the junta.

Initially Thailand, a historic enemy of Myanmar, offered help. The Thais were interested in logging and fishing rights in Myanmar. With the largest supply of teak in the world and no environmental regulation, Myanmar was the perfect partner for Thai firms, which worked closely with the military. Within the first few years, 47 companies would be involved in the logging exploitation in Myanmar. This mutually beneficial deal with Thailand devastated the ethnic insurgencies on the Thai border. The Karen and Mon fighters had been involved in the timber extraction to help finance their movements. The Thai military had no reason to give refuge to the exiles fleeing Myanmar. At times, the relationship between the Thai government and the military complicated the relationship with Myanmar. The situation remained tense with a continued lack of trust between the governments. Border skirmishes occurred between the tatmadaw and Thai military on several occasions. Thailand actually leveled harsh criticisms against the junta at the time of Myanmar's admission into the ASEAN in 1997. Still, most foreign policy experts in Thailand concluded that having a policy of "constructive engagement" with Myanmar was the pragmatic choice in a post–Cold War where counterbalancing Chinese regional influence was of paramount importance.

The newest partner working with the junta is India. Initially India had been a critic of the regime and its brutal human rights policy. For example, the government had awarded the Nehru Prize to Aung San Suu Kyi in 1995. As India emerged as a potential regional power, the government's priorities began to change. India's main concerns turned toward weapons sales, and exploitation of Myanmar's abundant natural resources. It became essential for India's geostrategic position to counter the growing Chinese influence over the junta. This change has allowed the Myanmar authorities to play India off against China.

Unquestionably, it has been the Chinese government that is most responsible for the continued intransigence of the military regime in Myanmar. Border trade between China and Myanmar has always been lucrative. As the insurgency issue quieted down, border profits soared. As Chinese regional influence increased in the post–Cold War period, Myanmar's relations with neighboring countries improved dramatically. Chinese trade in natural resources such as timber and gems increased in the 1990s. Chinese products entered the Myanmar markets, usually at the expense of Thai commodities.

Ethnic Han Chinese pushed into Myanmar with the hopes of reaping the economic benefits from the new open-door policy. Several urban areas saw a marked increase in the Chinese population. The net results unfortunately did not benefit the vast majority of Myanmar citizens. The junta's leadership derived the gains. Furthermore, the Buddhist influence was altered by the arrival of the Chinese. Offerings to the monks were reduced, leading to the decline of Buddhist influence in numerous urban centers. Furthermore, the dark side of globalization was apparent as cities became saturated with bars and a vibrant sex industry was flourishing.

The most significant area of Chinese influence was in national defense and military procurement. The junta's main weapons supplier was China. Everything from missiles, tanks, jet fighters, and trucks were purchased from China. Furthermore, Chinese leverage against insurgent groups was significant. This took pressure off of the regime and allowed them to concentrate on selective military targets. Finally, the Chinese were responsible for upgrading Myanmar's military infrastructure.

As long as the tatmadaw and Chinese shared a worldview regarding human rights, their relationship remains secured. Both countries cracked down on dissident behavior in the late 1980s. However, Myanmar and China were willing to disregard Western protests and opposition of their human rights violations. Neither would be isolated by their indifference to Western opposition regarding either democracy or human rights.

By the 1990s, increased calls for sanctions and boycotts dominated the discourse on Myanmar. Media attention became more focused on Myanmar's repressive policies, especially regarding the marquee figure Aung San Suu Kyi. Her notoriety in winning the Sakharov Peace Prize and later the Nobel Peace Prize made her one of the most recognized figures in Asia. This notoriety also helped build a stronger case for a more aggressive stance against the Myanmar authorities.

Limited economic sanctions were employed against the junta during the 1990s. The Clinton Administration halted direct investment in Myanmar in 1997. Activism regarding Myanmar became better organized and funded during the period directly after the announcement of Aung San Suu Kyi winning the Nobel Peace Prize. Groups such as Free Burma and the Burma Action Campaign led the public relations onslaught. The goal was to punish companies that invested in Myanmar.

The basic problem was that China, India, and several ASEAN countries continued to deal with the junta. Energy agreements were negotiated for the extraction of oil and natural gas. Myanmar's aggressive drilling polices led to the relocation and exploitation of ethnic minorities. Forced labor and the loss of property were commonplace.

Attempts at economic diversification failed in almost all cases. The tourism industry had the potential to generate considerable revenue. The "Visit Myanmar" campaign never met expectations for several reasons. First, the country simply did not have the infrastructure to deal effectively with the increase in tourism. Second, Aung San Suu Kyi and the NLD leadership called for westerners to institute a travel boycott until the junta agreed to negotiate in good faith with the NLD to form a coalition government.

DEALING WITH THE LADY: THE MILITARY STRUGGLE WITH AUNG SAN SUU KYI

Following the electoral fiasco, the junta had to find a way to effectively deal with Aung San Suu Kyi. It had always been stated to Suu Kyi that she could leave anytime to visit her husband and children with a clear understanding that she would never be allowed to return to Myanmar. On numerous occasions she had demanded to be treated like all other political prisoners and requested to be sent to the infamous Insein prison. The military instead opted to keep her under house arrest for most of her detention. Suu Kyi decided to go on a hunger strike in protest. After a period of 12 days and persistent pressure from her husband Michael Aris, Suu Kyi relented and ended the strike. After her family's departure in September 1989, all of their passports were revoked. Her husband would be allowed periodic visits, but the military was hoping that she would give up the fight and return to her family at some point in time.

As the pressure mounted on the NLD and Suu Kyi, the military also lashed out against the sangha. Over 300 monasteries were raided as the military regime decided to tighten the control over the Buddhist organizations within Myanmar. While incarcerated, Suu Kyi became devoted to strengthening her Buddhist faith. Her daily routine of meditation and memorizing the sutras gave her the inner strength to continue the fight.

Throughout her imprisonment, Suu Kyi was honored and her struggle was highly publicized. During the past 25 years she has received over 20 humanitarian awards. In 1991, she was awarded the Sakharov Prize for Freedom of Thought and later the announcement of the Nobel Peace Prize was made. This was a remarkable feat for someone who was involved in a political struggle for only a few brief years. Her sons Alex and Kim accepted it on her behalf in December 1991. The Nobel Prize was a mixed blessing for Aung San Suu Kyi. Demonstrations were organized on her behalf and an enormous amount of media attention was leveled in her direction. Suu Kyi was now a celebrity with Hollywood movies such as *Beyond Rangoon* and *The Lady* detailing her plight. The negative side was that the attention she received was looked upon in a critical fashion by the ruling junta. Many experts believed that the regime took an even harder stance in dealing with protesters and dissidents in order not to be perceived as weak in the eyes of the international community. The junta refused to allow former Nobel Peace Prize winners the Dalai Lama, Oscar Arias, Bishop Desmond Tutu, and Betty Williams enter Myanmar in order to meet with Suu Kyi. Their pleas for her release were of course ignored. She would later be awarded the Presidential Medal of Freedom by President Bill Clinton. A few years later the International Voices for Freedom event underscored the continued injustices in Myanmar. Artists such as U2, Paul McCartney, and REM have honored her in their music.

Suu Kyi was able to put together several publications during her incarceration. Her book *Freedom from Fear* was critically acclaimed and the proceeds from the book helped to keep her out of significant debt. Several writers interviewed Suu Kyi for publications. Ann Clemens wrote *The Voice of Hope*, based on a series of interviews conducted in the 1990s. *Letters from Burma* was a compilation of articles published by Suu Kyi. Additionally, the foreign media flocked to her residence, 54 University Avenue, in order to gain an interview or photograph of this larger than life symbol of democracy. Her calls for reconciliation with the junta were never seriously considered during this period.

On the occasions in which Suu Kyi was freed from house arrest, the junta quickly realized that she would not remain inactive or silent. The regime decided to organize well-paid gangs of thugs who operated under the name of the Union Solidarity and Development Association (USDA). They would use intimidation and violence to suppress any pro-democracy elements, NLD or others, from emerging in Myanmar. The tatmadaw continue to harass anyone suspected of opposing the government. Suu Kyi's attempts to visit areas outside of Rangoon were met with roadblocks and sometimes violent encounters with either military intelligence or members of the tatmadaw. In 1998, Suu Kyi was trapped inside of a car on two occasions, which led to her being forcibly removed from the vehicles by government authorities.

Suu Kyi's husband had been banned from visiting her in Myanmar because he supposedly smuggled her speeches out of the country on previous visits. In 1998, tragedy was to strike Suu Kyi in the most personal way. Her husband and source of strength for so many years was diagnosed with prostate cancer. His pleas to be allowed to visit his wife prior to his death fell on deaf ears. The junta probably felt this was the best opportunity to rid Myanmar of "the lady" as the international community now called her. The regime monitored their phone conversations and began cutting them off when she was on the line with her husband. This cruel tactic was meant to inflict the maximum pain and suffering on Suu Kyi. She had no intention of leaving Myanmar to visit her dying husband. Aris passed away on March 27, 1999.

The struggle between Suu Kyi and the junta continued unabated. It was turning into a war of endurance between the generals and what remained of the democratic opposition. Suu Kyi's next step was to attempt to break free from Rangoon by traveling around drumming up support for what seemed at times an undefined cause. The military would stop her with roadblocks and either wait her out or at times force the vehicle to return to Rangoon. The military claimed to be protecting Suu Kyi from hostile crowds and possible violence. Eventually Suu Kyi would be placed under house arrest again. This second round of house arrest would last 19 months.

During the tumultuous early part of 2002, Than Shwe uncovered a plot against the regime. Members of Ne Win's family were implicated. A few weeks later, a thaw between the pro-democracy movement and the generals emerged. Subsequently, Japan cancelled Myanmar's debt, an act that may have been part of a deal to release Suu Kyi. Under Suu Kyi's guidance, democracy workshops were organized in close proximity to her residence. Only after patently waiting for months for some sort of positive response from the generals to participate in a meaningful dialogue did Suu Kyi make the decision to once again venture out of the capital.

Residents of the regions Suu Kyi would travel to were warned not to venture out to hear her speak. She traveled to the predominately Muslim area of Arakan. The military would place roadblocks or wire across the travel routes. Furthermore, the USDA members were out in force in order to intimidate residents and harass Suu Kyi's supporters. Suu Kyi ventured to the northern area of Myanmar visiting the Chin, Kachin, and Shan states. She now traveled with a larger contingent of bodyguards. Military intelligence was always out documenting and photographing the rallies. The pro-democracy movement seemed to be gathering support, to the dismay of the junta.

At Depayin, the ultimate clash would ensue. Well-armed USDA forces and members of the military ambushed Suu Kyi's entourage. This attack was carefully orchestrated and planned. Nearly a week prior to the attack, Lieutenant Colonel Than Han had gathered local USDA members to the campus of Depayin High School. Several days of training ensued in preparation for the assault. The assailants were armed with bamboo staves, baseball bats, and sharpened iron rods, many of the weapons prepared by a local blacksmith. Years later it was confirmed that this event was indeed meant to culminate in the assassination of Aung San Suu Kyi. It is estimated that close to 5,000 pro-government forces were in place for what turned out to be a massacre. It was labeled "Black Friday" and over 70 people were beaten to death and over 100 injured. Witnesses later claimed that the attackers seemed to be drunk or on drugs during the carnage. No mercy was shown even to women and children, who were beaten as well. The evidence was quickly removed as police quickly began arresting suspected sympathizers. Former secretary of the USDA U Win Sein later stated that Than Shwe had stated that the attack was meant to "get rid of" and "exterminate" Suu Kyi. When members of the security forces present at the meeting questioned the meaning of the statements, Shwe supposedly replied, "We must exterminate her." Within hours, Suu Kyi and other leaders of the NLD were once again arrested.

A committee investigating the Depayin massacre, cochaired by U Khin Kyaw Han, a member of parliament from the NLD, stated that no such coordinated attack could have taken place without the total backing and planning of the security and military apparatus in Myanmar. Several eyewitness accounts have confirmed Than Shwe's precise role in the attempted assassination.

What makes the Depayin massacre so heroic is that throughout the carnage the NLD and Aung San Suu Kyi's supporters stood steadfast in their nonviolent approach. As supporters were beaten mercilessly, they surrounded Suu Kyi in layers to attempt to protect her from the mob violence. The split-second decision of her driver to speed up as the windows of her car were being broken as well as his decision to drive through the roadblock setup by the military inevitably saved her life.

As has been the case for decades, the military regime attempted to ignore the international outcry. This was difficult as new sanctions were implemented and the regime was showing signs of fatigue over the pressure exerted from the international community. Suu Kyi would spend several months in the Insein prison before being put under house arrest. Even after the horrific event, Suu Kyi was quoted as saying that she was still willing to turn the page and use the situation as an opportunity for dialogue. Unfortunately, the unsuccessful attempt to assassinate Suu Kyi created a larger rift within the ruling junta, leading to further distrust and anxiety within the leadership. Than Shwe claimed that her continued presence created a significant threat to the peace and stability of Myanmar. He claimed that her actions were a threat to national security.

The failed attempt on Aung San Suu Kyi's life put Than Shwe in a position of weakness. Khin Nyunt was now put in charge of trying to rehabilitate the regime's image. The most significant aspect of the rehabilitation was the announcement of the seven-point road map to democracy. This document was to be the guide to the political future of Myanmar that would ultimately lead to democratization. Several secret talks were held between members of the junta and NLD representatives, in particular Than Tun. According to defector Aung Lynn Htut, a final agreement was in place by the spring of 2004. Ultimately the negotiations were futile because Than Shwe rejected the tentative agreement reached between the government representatives and the NLD negotiation team. It was apparent that Than Shwe still had solid control over the decision-making process. This episode led to a final power struggle between Than Shwe and Khin Nyunt. While away on a trip to Singapore, Nyunt's headquarters was raided and evidence of an illicit trade network was uncovered. In October 2004, Nyunt was arrested and subsequently put on trial on corruption charges. This event solidified the status quo until the breakthrough of 2010–2011.

FROM RANGOON TO NAYPYIDAW: THE RELOCATION OF MYANMAR'S CAPITAL

Rangoon has served as the capital of Myanmar since early in the colonial era. As the largest urban area in the country, it was a natural location for the center of government. A monumental change occurred at 6:37 A.M. on November 6, 2005, as hundreds of government servants left Rangoon in trucks, shouting, "We are leaving! We are leaving!" On November 11, a second massive convoy departed, carrying military battalions and government ministers. This move, probably influenced by astrologers and extreme paranoia, was a shock to nearly everyone in the country. Government officials were given two days notice.

The massive construction of the new capital cost billions of dollars. The location was in a remote malaria-infested area in central Myanmar near the town of Pyinmana. Than Shwe called the capital Naypyidaw, meaning "seat of kings." Foreign diplomats were informed of the move several days after it occurred. A simple fax number was given to the diplomats if they needed to reach the government. Members of the civil service within Myanmar were also frustrated and angered over such an irrational move. Even for a regime that tended to gravitate toward the bizarre, this was considered extreme. The isolationist's tendencies of the regime were increasing.

Discussions about relocation of the capital or at least some of the administrative components of the state were informally discussed as early as 1998. The initial idea, however, was simply to move the military headquarters to a different location and not the entire administrative structure. This proposed move was meant to clearly separate the military and civilian components of the state. The move was to coincide with the completion of the national convention. When General Khin Nyunt was removed from his position in the government, the decision to relocate the entire apparatus was apparently made.

Several possible factors played into the decision. First, the regime felt that Rangoon was a security threat from both internal and external forces. Internally, the regime feared a repeat of the 1988 protests, which under the right circumstances could bring down the government. Externally, there was growing fear that an international force or an American invasion was within the realm of possibility. The new location was supposedly more secure and fortifiable. The regime had developed an intricate series of tunnels and "rat holes" to secure the leadership in case of invasion. Second, Rangoon was an aging city with infrastructural problems. The regime may have decided that the refurbishing of the historical capital was not worth the investment. A third factor was that the regime and its forces would have quick access to volatile insurgent areas such as the Shan, Chin, and Karen states. This scenario seems unlikely because of the diminishing threat from ethnic and religious insurgents. Fourth, the generals may have been following a pattern developed in precolonial times in which kings had relocated the capital at particular historical moments. A final factor was that fortunetellers had encouraged the key members of the junta to move the capital. This somewhat bizarre theory has strong support. On multiple occasions in modern Myanmar history fortunetellers have impacted governmental policy. Whatever the actual reason this type of move for a country with immense socioeconomic problems was totally irrational.

13

Political Turmoil and Natural Catastrophe, 2007–2008

Following the relocation of the capital to Naypyidaw in late 2005, the political system in Myanmar seemed to be in a holding pattern. The regime, however, was drifting further out of touch with the average citizen. On August 15, 2007, the Myanmar authorities unexpectedly removed all subsidies on fuel and natural gas prices as well as basic commodities. The increase of natural gas prices in some places was an astronomical 500 percent. Fuel and diesel costs doubled. This had a devastating impact on the already significantly impoverished population in Myanmar. This increase shocked the citizens of Myanmar, threatening the livelihood of the majority of the population. An earlier price hike in 2005 did not spark any protests, giving the regime a sense of confidence in pushing through an additional hike. The results were far different. A spontaneous outbreak of protests occurred as a result. A larger percentage of the population was living at or below the subsistence level in 2007. Wages were not increasing to keep up with the growing rate of inflation. Many of the workers were falling below the subsistence level. The laborers who commuted long distances to the urban areas were devastated as the price of bus tickets, taxis, and other forms of transportation were hit the hardest. Also the fuel needed for cooking increased substantially.

The spike in fuel prices led to numerous protests. On August 19, an estimated 500 people gathered for a march in Tamwe township of Rangoon to
protest the fuel price increase. Prominent "Burma Watch Groups" claimed
that this was the largest public demonstration in years. The 88-generation pro-
democracy activists mostly organized the early protests. On August 21, the
government responded by arresting prominent activists, targeting most of
the leadership of the 88-generation student movement. By the 25th, more than
100 people had been detained, including leaders of the NLD and other leaders of civil society organizations. The state-controlled media began to publi-
cize the detentions, claiming that the agitators were attempting to undermine
peace and security within Myanmar. The state also claimed that this was an
attempt to destabilize the ongoing national convention process.

Almost immediately protesters were harassed and threatened by the pro-
government Union Solidarity Development Association (USDA) and other
militias that were armed by government agents. By August 22, armed police,
who assisted the USDA members in assaulting the civilians, interrupted additional protests. The police later arrested protesters following clashes with
the USDA contingent.

A key turning point for the Saffron Revolution occurred on August 28 when
monks in Sittwe (located in the Arakan state) took to the streets. On the same
day, labor organizers led by Su Su Nway marched in Rangoon chanting for
lower fuel and commodity prices. The regime's reprisals became increasingly
violent in early September. The fact that the government was in the process of
announcing the completion of the 14-year-long national convention in early
September may have played into the decision to crackdown in such an aggressive fashion.

Another turning point in the Saffron Revolution occurred on September 5.
The religious center of Pakokku, situated close to Mandalay, became a center
of protest for the monks. The monks denounced the previous price hikes and
were able to gain significant momentum from area residents. The decision by
the monks to join the protests was deeply significant because of the unique
moral standing that is placed on the sangha. Furthermore, since colonial times
monks have been at the center of political uprisings in Burma.

The military launched into a brutal crackdown against the monks at this
time. Monks were tied to lampposts and brutally beaten. Dozens of monks
and bystanders were apprehended and imprisoned. Furthermore, it was ru-
mored that one monk died as a result of the violence. This abuse of the monks
created significant backlash against the regime. Protests spread and the anger
against the regime reached a breaking point. The following day a government
delegation was sent to the monastery to seek forgiveness for the actions of
the previous day. The delegation also encouraged the leadership at the monastery to stop further protests from occurring. The tension actually escalated

as protesters gathered outside burning the cars of government officials. The 1,000-strong crowd demanded detained protesters from the previous day be released. Eventually the officials escaped after a nearly six-hour standoff. State-controlled media denounced the monks' action and they were blamed for the outbreak of hostilities. Warnings were issued that any further protest attempts would not be tolerated. A reference was made that a repeat of the events of 1988 would not occur.

The Pakokku incident led to the formation of the All Burma Monks Alliance (ABMA). A statement was issued by the new organization on September 9, giving the State Peace and Development Council (SPDC) a week to comply with several demands or face a religious boycott.

New forces were emerging to oppose the regime by 2007. Social activists concerned with economic and social problems rather than the traditional and older pro-democracy movements were appearing. Furthermore, many of the 88-generation student activists had been released from prison and started to reform old network connections by the time of the 2007 price hike. Within the first week following the price increase, over 100 demonstrators were arrested. The government goal was a broader crackdown as residences were searched and documents seized. At times, the junta used militias hired by the USDA. International media outlets began to cover the events, which initially were not that substantial.

The newly formed ABMA issued a challenge to the regime. First, the authorities were to apologize for the Pakokku fiasco. Second, all political prisoners, including Aung San Suu Kyi, were to be released. Third, fuel and commodity prices had to be reduced. Finally, a dialogue was to be opened to promote national reconciliation. The deadline was to coincide with the anniversary of the brutal crackdown by State Law and Order Restoration Council in 1988.

The regime attempted to divide the protest movement. Attempts to buy off the loyalty of monasteries with financial gifts were made, but by and large failed. The crackdown continued and the public relations campaign accelerated as the SPDC attempted to vilify the movement. The state-run media claimed that forces were working to attempt to ferment revolution and cause internal disruptions within the state. The hype went as far as to accuse the protesters of terrorism supported by the West, most notably the United States. The regime's next move was to cut communication services by deactivating landlines and mobile phone services of key activists' locations. A further step was taken to establish military tribunals at Insein prison to retaliate against several labor activists. Harsh prison terms were issued to multiple activists. The next step taken was to start counter protest by pro-government activists. Mass rallies were organized to celebrate the completion of the national convention. Attendance was mandatory in many areas of the country.

After the regime refused to meet the demands of the monks, the ABMA released a statement on September 14 that would have monumental implications.

The monks excommunicated government officials through the overturning of the alms bowl. This process is known as *Patta Nikkujjana Kamma*. Peaceful protests were encouraged by the religious leadership.

The issuing of the boycott would have serious implications in such a predominately Buddhist society. The giving and receiving of alms is considered a vitally important act in Buddhism. The gaining of merit would be denied to the military and regime.

An important element of the boycott was the perceived threat to the legitimacy of the regime. For decades the SPDC and its supporters had sought to cultivate an image of protectors of the sangha. Part of the public relations apparatus of the regime was ceremonies that focused on merit making. Included in this would be gifts to monasteries, pagoda-restoration projects and numerous appearances with clergy, and the holding of the World Buddhist Conference. The boycott was a dangerous challenge to the regime, which was rarely seen in the modern history of Myanmar. On September 21, the ABMA issued a statement denouncing the military dictatorship as the enemy of the citizens. The alliance called for the evil regime to be banished from Burmese soil forever.

An earlier attempt in 1990 by the monks to combat the regime had led to dissolution of illegal monk organizations and unions, and a declaration that any monk who took part in nonreligious activities would be expelled from the sangha and imprisoned. Over 100 monasteries were raided in subsequent days, but efforts to mold the sangha into a pro-government entity were for the most part unsuccessful.

After the failure of the regime to reply, the ABMA started the excommunication process on September 17. Rallying calls by the ABMA were met with enthusiastic support for the sangha as further protests were announced. Initial protests were allowed to occur with little or no government interference. On September 18, approximately 300 monks gathered at the Shwedagon pagoda in Yangon. The significance of the location (a historical focal point of opposition) led the tatmadaw to block the protesters who moved to the downtown area. When the monks moved to gather at the Sule pagoda the government forces did not intervene. Several hundred citizens joined in the protests at this point. By this time, the authorities were starting to document, photograph, and videotape the protest activities.

Protests were occurring in numerous cities, such as Pegu, where over 1,000 monks protested. In Sittwe, monks protested calling for a lowering of the price of commodities. By the end of the day, lay people had joined with monks as the crowd swelled to over 10,000. Sporadic violence broke out and onlookers documented some police brutality.

During the next 48 hours the protesters did not encounter police brutality, but plainclothes officers videotaped the majority of protest activities. It was apparent to the regime that the protests were becoming more widespread with activities in Sittwe, Prome, and Mandalay. The uncertainty on the part of the security apparatus is difficult to explain. The authorities may have been taken by surprise or the authorities may have believed that the protests would die down after a few days. What is known is that momentum was building on the side of the resistance as the numbers swelled nationwide. As students joined the monks, it was clearly stated that if they were to be involved in the protest it was to continue in a peaceful manner.

September 22 saw a significant shift in the movement. As the protests were rapidly growing, a group of monks made it through barricades around the house of Aung San Suu Kyi. The steel gate to enter her courtyard was opened and she was allowed to greet the protesters from behind a cordon of police guards with riot shields. The image of "the lady" tearing up as protesters chanted the *metta sutta* Buddhist prayers was probably the high point of the Saffron Revolution. The photo of Suu Kyi (the first time in four years that she had been seen in public) made international headlines. This turned what had been a mostly religious movement into a political event. The protesters gained momentum and courage from seeing Suu Kyi.

By September 23, the protests in Rangoon increased to over 20,000, making it the largest gathering since the crackdown of 1988. The tone of the protests had turned more political as chants for the release of Aung San Suu Kyi grew in intensity. The security forces did not allow a repeat of the previous day as they stopped the gathering from approaching her compound again.

Over 100,000 protesters gathered in Yangon on September 24. This was now a truly national movement including students, political opposition figures, and famous personalities. Several political organizations that had been banned began to resurface. Chants for political prisoners to be freed became the center-piece of the activity. The red fighting peacock, a symbol of the resistance, started to reemerge. In all, 25 cities had sustained protests on September 24.

The first announcement by the government occurred on the evening of September 24. General Maung condemned the protests. The regime believed the goal of the protesters was to harm national development and stability. The government-controlled state sangha committee began a process of taking control of all Buddhists affairs. Directive 93 prohibited monks from participating in secular affairs, which amounted to banning the monks from further involvement in the protest movement. Monks and novices were also banned from joining organizations deemed illegal, such as ABMA.

The directive was part of a process that had been used numerous times in Myanmar's history to prosecute protesters and impose harsh prison terms. A more-noted police presence was in place during the evening of September 24. By the following morning, the change in tone was continuing. Additional police forces were moved into key areas and loudspeakers blared out warnings not to engage in any further protests. The nonviolent protests continued and the addition of the "fighting peacock," a symbol from the 1988 movement, was in full view. A joint statement from the 88-generation students and the ABMA was issued encouraging the release of political prisoners, economic reforms, and national reconciliation. The protesters were determined to continue in spite of the possibility of harsh reprisals.

Late in the evening of September 25, authorities began to arrest some of the prominent public figures who had come out to support the protest movement. Opposition politician U Win Naing and comedian Zargana were both detained that evening. Other high-profile citizens went into hiding at this time. The military moved in large numbers, occupying parts of Rangoon. Riot police also were deployed in key strategic positions.

The eastern side of Shwedagon pagoda bore the brunt of a major onslaught from the riot police and military units. General Khin Ye oversaw the operation. Barbed wire barricades were placed in the entrance to the pagoda. Monks were detained and the crowds that gathered grew more anxious. Shortly after, teargas and violent action commenced. The riot police cracked down on the protesters in a brutal fashion. Monks and student were beaten relentlessly. The riot police beat and took into detention trapped monks, who fled back to the monastery. Evidence of the ordeal was quickly removed as the regime cleaned the areas of blood and debris. Key intersections were blocked, making any further organized resistance difficult. The area around Thakin Mya Park saw some of the heaviest casualties during the first day of the crackdown. Live ammunition was used against protesters who decided to sit in the streets chanting Buddhists prayers as part of the protest. Bodies would be quickly carted off, following a pattern that would be repeated frequently. The following day a curfew was implemented and the security forces raided monasteries and arrested Buddhist leaders. During the cover of night, multiple raids took place, which included the looting and destruction of numerous monasteries. Citizens were outraged, but could do little to stop the onslaught by the military and police. By the morning of September 27, massive arrests were recorded and multiple injuries and fatalities resulted. The response escalated quickly as the military, rather than police authorities, took control over quelling the protests. An essential part of the tatmadaw's plan was to lessen the influence of the monks in the protest movement. The initial step of closing monasteries and keeping the monks away from the mass movement was significant in stifling the momentum of the protest.

The crackdown became more violent as live rounds became commonplace. At the Sule pagoda in downtown Rangoon, the crowds chanted "the army is the army of Aung San for the people, not to kill the people and the monks." Eventually the military opened fire, killing first with rubber bullets and then with live ammunition. The most high-profile event was the execution of a

Japanese video-journalist Kenji Nagai in Yangon. The military ordered the people to scatter or be shot. As the violence intensified, plain-clothed thugs working for the authorities participated in the violence against the protesters. The protesters remained peaceful throughout the bloody ordeal. The wounded received no medical attention.

By September 30, the regime was able to subdue the remaining protests. The crackdown was successful due to the work by the civilian thugs who were paid by the regime, as well as the combined forces of police and military. During the final days of September, nighttime raids of monasteries intensified. The destruction of religious property was significant. Numerous monks were ordered to de-robe and return to civilian life. Thousands of monks were detained in Yangon, Sittwe, and Kachin. During the military sweep, monks were physically abused, put through extended interrogation, and constantly humiliated. Tracking down the monks involved in the movement was made easier by the intense surveillance undertaken during the early days of the protests. The authorities resorted to detaining family and friends of wanted suspects. The once-vibrant Buddhist city of Yangon was especially hard hit and it was virtually emptied of clergy during the crackdown.

Authorities also took the drastic step of severing the Internet in Myanmar to ensure that Western media outlets could no longer receive information on the brutal suppression of the population. Detention centers were set up in major urban centers in Myanmar. Torture and human rights abuses were commonplace. The notorious Insein prison was used as one of the main detention and torture centers. Some of the documented abuses included inhumane conditions in the cells, severe beatings, sleep deprivation, and torture. Amnesty International and Human Rights Watch later documented the extent of the brutality. The curfews remained in place for several weeks as the regime continued to hunt down anyone and everyone involved in the Saffron Revolution.

Subsequently, the regime crushed any signs of dissent. The use of photographic and video footage to identify protesters was especially effective. Thousands of civilians (many not involved whatsoever in the uprising) were detained, questioned, and in many cases tortured. On the surface, the regime seemed to have suppressed the movement, but the underlying current remained. The brutality in which the sangha was treated and the unbelievable destruction of monasteries guaranteed that intense resentment remained.

The image of the army probably hit an all-time low following the Saffron Revolution. Throughout the history of Myanmar, governments have always sought legitimacy through the sangha and the level of violence used against the monks has damaged the relationship permanently.

The international community responded with near-universal condemnation of the Myanmar authorities. Even Asian nations that usually are more muted in condemning the regime spoke out in protest. Singapore (speaking on behalf of the entire ASEAN body) expressed revulsion over the violence against the monks. Even China, the main ally of the regime, issued a statement calling for a peaceful resolution to the crisis. Finally, the United Nations Security Council issued a presidential statement deploring the violence against peaceful protesters. The UN Human Rights Council called for the release of political prisoners and national reconciliation among the parties.

As far as specific tangible actions to be taken, the international community differs. Several Western powers, including the United States and Canada, pushed for new sanctions to try and force policy change by the SPDC. Most of Asian countries, including all of Myanmar's neighbors, oppose such punitive action. The rationale behind not taking action is that it would undermine diplomatic efforts and diminish international influence overall. The middle path is taken by the EU and Japan, which want a more carrot-and-stick approach with targeted sanctions in combination with incentives to reform. The overall lack of international resolve regarding tangible action weakens the ability of global powers to influence outcomes.

The implications of the Saffron Revolution are considerable. Internationally, the regime's brutality was once again on public display. Condemnation was widespread as the protest crackdown was front-page news globally. The brutality against the Buddhist community in Myanmar was excessive even by the standards of the junta. This could have negative implications for the legitimacy of the regime both internally and externally. Economically, businesses were hurt by the upheaval and tourism suffered considerably. Many business elites were unhappy with the way the regime handled the crisis. This lack of confidence among the business elites and clergy could have potential ramifications. Finally, an economy already suffering from the fuel hike of August was further damaged.

FROM MAN-MADE DISASTER TO NATURAL DISASTER: CYCLONE NARGIS

During May 2 to 3, 2008, Myanmar was devastated by a category-four cyclone. Named Nargis, this cyclone was the worst natural disaster in the recorded history of Myanmar. The storm with 200-mile winds carved a path of destruction through the Ayeyarwaddy delta, as well as Yangon and parts of the Mon state. Literally hundreds of villages were instantaneously leveled and the agricultural lands lay in ruin. The actual death toll may never be known, but most estimates put the number around the 140,000 mark. An additional 2.4 million citizens were affected by the loss of homes or livelihood. The post-Nargis joint assessment (PONJA) puts the number of displaced at 800,000. The infrastructure of the areas hit was obliterated. Electricity, communications, transportation, education, and health care networks, all sustained massive damage.

The damage to the economy was compounded by the fact that the Ayeyarwaddy delta is the main food-producing area in Myanmar. Additionally, Yangon is the industrial and commercial center of the country. PONJA estimates that the economic loss is valued at 4 billion dollars, which is 21 percent of national gross domestic product (GDP). For the Ayeyarwaddy area, it is 74 percent, while in Yangon the estimated GDP loss is 57 percent. Economic rehabilitation will take years even with extensive external assistance. The potential for political and social upheaval will increase as citizens move to less vulnerable areas. Furthermore, pressure on the government increased as more and more citizens fell below the subsistence level.

By virtually all accounts, the government failed miserably in responding to cyclone Nargis. The PONJA report painted a distorted picture of the efforts of the regime. The government claimed that after the cyclone struck, both the SPDC and Myanmar's army assisted in relief efforts. The regime claimed to help with relief supplies, medical care, infrastructural repair, and reestablishing security. Eyewitness testimonies state that the reality was much different. It was obvious that the tatmadaw was the only organization in Myanmar with the manpower, resources, and communication ability to deal with such a catastrophe. Not only did the junta fail to respond in a timely manner, but they also stalled any sort of international assistance from initially reaching the most vulnerable areas devastated. The local authorities were unsuccessful in coordinating action. Corruption also plagued the initial efforts as authorities kept relief supplies, selling them on the black market. This illegal action included diversion of donated goods for resale and forced labor being performed by villagers. Camp conditions were appalling with little or no aid going to victims. The SPDC seemed to focus more on maintaining law and order rather than assisting those in need.

Foreign workers were continually denied access to the victims. Many of the aid organizations were stuck in the urban areas, such as Yangon, for long periods of time. The regime hampered efforts and set up obstacles throughout the early stages of the process. The international community expressed continued frustration at the regime's lack of effort and concern and urged the regime to accept international assistance. A full two weeks after the cyclone hit, aid was still not making it to the Ayeyarwaddy region.

The United Nations was informed on May 23 that aid workers would be allowed into the areas hit by Nargis. The announcement was met with skepticism from observers who felt the regime was trying to deflect criticism and secure more money. The SPDC continued to restrict access to most areas. The UN Human Rights Council passed a resolution calling on the government to allow immediate, full, and unhindered access. Approximately 200 UN staff members were allowed to visit affected areas, but the numbers were so small as to make the impact minimal. By mid June, only about half of the affected people had received any assistance.

Internal assistance from activists, celebrities, monks, and ordinary citizens was organized early on. Unfortunately, the SPDC also blocked these internal efforts to mitigate the suffering. Restrictions were put in place and anyone visiting the devastated areas was closely monitored. Ultimately, any direct aid from internal sources was forbidden. Local organizations were informed not to cooperate with monks trying to deliver any assistance. The government ended any aid delivery very quickly, claiming that assistance would create a level of dependency on the part of the citizens impacted by the disaster.

Harassment of relief workers was also commonplace and the comedian Zargana was arrested in Yangon in early June. Several dozen activists would be arrested by the end of the month for attempting to deliver aid to affected regions. The regime even utilized civilian thugs to brutalize volunteers attempting to establish an aid convoy.

The Myanmar government was also involved in serious misappropriation of aid. Assistance was diverted for resale or other illicit purposes. There were numerous episodes of authorities confiscating donated items that were sent to the Naypyidaw or sold at market places. In some cases, victims were charged for the assistance they received. Another ploy used by the regime was requiring a "yes" vote on the national referendum in order for aid to be handed out. Theft was commonplace at all levels of the military. Essential items for survival were confiscated, including mosquito netting, filters for water, tents, soap, stoves, and blankets. An additional problem was the distorted money exchange rates that benefitted the military regime. Over 10 million in aid may have been lost because of manipulation of money exchange rates.

The camp system established by the government was dismal. Food was inadequate and travel was restricted, leading to bribes being paid by cyclone survivors in order to be let out of the camps. The camp situation was also used to organize voter intimidation for the upcoming national referendum regarding the country's draft constitution on May 24. Survivors were told that a "yes" vote was required in order to receive assistance and aid. By mid June, most camps were shut down as the referendum was completed and citizens were forced to return to their villages.

Medical assistance was also lacking following Nargis. Medical support was delayed and numerous teams had visas cancelled for no apparent reason. This obstruction was especially costly to the children of Myanmar who were in desperate need of medicine and treatment.

An additional problem concerned the treatment of the dead. Identification and burial of the dead was not a high priority for the regime. Reports from witnesses on the ground stated that dead bodies continued to float in waterways several months after the cyclone hit. This contaminated the water supply and also caused significant mental health problems for villagers across the country. The regime went as far as to arrest volunteers attempting to bury victims.

Another problem encountered by the citizens of Myanmar was land confiscation. All land in the country is owned by the state, which allows the citizens to use the land as long as they continue to use it in productive ways. In order to expedite the return of villagers to their land after the cyclone, the regime began to confiscate lands not being utilized. In some cases, the land was given to large agribusiness firms, which paid the regime for the property. These large-scale agricultural entities forced the small farmers out of existence, threatening thousands of citizens. Many citizens that returned to their land were forced to rent tractors and equipment at exorbitant rates well beyond the means of the average peasant farmer.

The establishment of camps also made the population more vulnerable in numerous ways. Human trafficking and the recruitment of child soldiers were two of the more problematic areas of concern. Young girls orphaned were reported to be offering sex for money. The issue of sexually transmitted disease and the personal safety of the girls was a grave concern. In addition, it was feared that the military would use the situation to recruit more children into the army. According to international organizations, including the UN, Myanmar is actively engaged in child-soldier recruitment. It was also reported that the orphanages set up by the Myanmar authorities were like prisons. Efforts by community leaders to keep the children gathered together outside of the government-run institutions was met with hostility from the state. Many adoptions were facilitated to military families so that the orphans would eventually end up as part of the military establishment.

The psychological impact of cyclone Nargis cannot be overlooked. For survivors, the images of the horrific event will not be forgotten. Emma Larkin in her groundbreaking work *Everything Is Broken* recounts a survivor story, "In a village not far from the delta town of Mawlamyainggyun, I walked past a large drinking water pond that seemed to me a beautiful and tranquil spot. It was early morning and vivid pink lotus buds were opening on the surface of the water. But the villagers shuddered as they passed it. Many dead bodies had been found floating in the pond after cyclone Nargis and, no matter how many times it was cleaned and washed out with lime powder, people still found that the water had a peculiar taste." (196).

THE PERSPECTIVE OF THE MYANMAR AUTHORITIES

It has been argued that the harsh criticism leveled against the regime is somewhat overstated. The government's actions generated a high level of criticism, as global leaders grew frustrated over the lack of cooperation and regard for human life. The disaster was unprecedented in the history of

Myanmar. The authorities in Myanmar felt that the international community quickly politicized the crisis to harm the standing of the regime. In addition, the fact that the military was undergoing a generational change may have also complicated relief efforts. The fact that this transition was taking place may have caused confusion and panic within the new authority structure. Low-level authorities may have been fearful of making any substantive decision.

In addition, Myanmar was coming out of the turmoil of the 2007 Saffron Revolution. The relationship between the regime and the international community became more contentious based on the criticism leveled at the regime following the brutal crackdown against political protesters and monks. The paranoia of the regime was most evident in how they handled the media and information on the crisis. Significant restrictions were placed on the media throughout the ordeal.

The cyclone hitting one week prior to the planned constitutional referendum also created enormous problems. All of the government's attention was focused on this seminal event that was the cornerstone of the transitional plan. The decision of the regime to go forward with the process (even though it was delayed in some areas) was condemned by the entire international community. It showed a callous indifference to the suffering of the people at a critical time in the history of Myanmar. Most believed the referendum was a farce with the outcome never in doubt.

To make matters worse, the government blocked initial attempts by international aid organizations to assist in relief efforts. The government agents in different regions were at times given conflicting orders, further confusing an already chaotic situation. It also was apparent that the authorities did not want aid workers to enter the hardest-hit areas around the Ayeyarwaddy delta. Military roadblocks were setup and access to the delta remained restricted. It should be added that even in the best of times, access to the remote delta areas is problematic. The tatmadaw was also in the process of a generational change and institutional restructuring. This factor may have slowed down the decision-making process down considerably. The timing of the disaster, less than eight months after the Saffron Revolution, led to the military perception to deal with this as a security problem rather than a humanitarian concern. Furthermore, the lack of experts with the necessary technical skills hampered the operational effectiveness.

Internal assistance from citizens was also rejected as the government confiscated supplies and refused most citizens' requests to enter the areas hit. Several arrests were made of private citizens accused of subversive activities for attempting to help in cyclone relief. It was speculated that supplies left with the military never reached the affected areas. Myanmar authorities denied requests from the United States, Britain, and France to deliver supplies to the areas affected. Had the authorities in Myanmar allowed supplies to be transported to the military airport at Bathein, aid would have reached the population much quicker. The international community was also concerned that the death toll could rise due to disease and starvation.

Within days, full-blown condemnation of the regime was airing. Foreign ministers and international dignitaries spoke out against the junta's seeming indifference to the suffering of the population. This rhetoric was for the most part empty because of a guaranteed Chinese veto of any action proposed against Myanmar. This may have actually increased the paranoia levels of the junta in Naypyidaw, leading to even further delays by the authorities. Media access was significantly restricted as the government arrested anyone attempting to provide footage of the affected areas. The junta felt that a sudden influx of foreigners could loosen their grip on power. Monitoring the international aid workers would also be difficult.

The regime considered this humanitarian disaster to be a serious security threat. The potential for social unrest and the breakdown of order was very critical. The fear of international relief workers fermenting further unrest and revolution was a concern for the regime. Reestablishing order and stability was the top priority for the government. The threat of Western soldiers establishing a presence in Myanmar was considered unacceptable. The public statement of the French Foreign Minister Bernard Kouchner calling for the use of the UN Security Council to authorize military intervention to secure access for relief aid under the principle of "responsibility to protect" created significant alarm in Naypyidaw. In addition, during a White House briefing, First Lady Laura Bush launched an attack on the regime for failing to warn the population beforehand or to take a more aggressive stance in helping with aid and assistance. She also called on neighboring countries to influence political change in Myanmar.

Many international observers believe that the dysfunctional nature of the regime played into the inability to take action. The response of the regime parallels how the North Korean government dealt with the famine a decade earlier. Myanmar authorities lacked the experience and technological knowhow to deal with the relief efforts. Power outages, lack of computer access, and general bureaucratic inefficiency were all occurring in Myanmar.

Critics of the Myanmar policy argued that the cost of disengagement is too severe to overlook. The country is left more vulnerable to future disasters because of the lack of assistance from international donors. Furthermore, not only are they more vulnerable to the initial shock, but they also have less capacity to cope with the aftermath. Western policies limit aid to just a few dollars per capita, which is considerably less than the average for less developed countries. These criticisms state that the West has sacrificed opportunities to promote economic reform and empower local communities by taking a hardline stance against the junta.

The government's lack of experience in dealing with foreign aid workers and the lack of trust on the part of the regime made a very difficult situation much worse. The ambitious push by Western aid organizations may have alienated the regime, which already felt hesitant about letting perceived enemies of the state access to the stricken areas.

By late May, more substantive aid was finally starting to arrive. The entry visa process became more streamlined as bureaucratic efficiency increased. Ban Ki-moon met with Than Shwe, helping to lessen the tension between the junta and international authorities. However, the claims of too little too late would continue to echo in any critique of the disaster relief.

In addition, the regime stifled any sort of collective remembrance or memorialization. The regime's gag orders on all public forums left the citizens only a private avenue to mourn and remember the catastrophe. One of the great tragedies in the modern history of Myanmar is that recent historical events are not allowed to be remembered or acknowledged in any significant way.

14

Contemporary Myanmar: Optimism and Caution

The constitutional referendum went forward although it was delayed in 47 of the most significantly affected areas. Media coverage of the referendum was overwhelming, and the plight of the suffering peasants impacted by Nargis was overlooked. The results announced by the State Peace and Development Council (SPDC) were an overwhelming 92 percent voting in favor of the constitution. The government claimed a clear mandate to move forward toward democratic elections scheduled for 2010.

A VISITOR COMPLICATES MATTERS

A bizarre turn of events dominated Myanmar during the summer of 2009. On May 3, American John Yettaw, a devout Mormon from Missouri swam across Lake Inlay and arrived at the residence of Aung San Suu Kyi. After warning her of a possible assassination attempt, the obviously deranged Yettaw was reluctantly permitted to stay at the house for two evenings. This was an act of compassion on behalf of Aung San Suu Kyi as Yettaw was both physically and mentally not well. This was actually the second time Yettaw had attempted to see Suu Kyi. An earlier attempt had failed and Myanmar security personnel had turned him back. At the time of his successful arrival, the 53-year-old American was in fragile health as he suffered from diabetes and epileptic seizures. After departing from the house, Yettaw was detained and later charged by the authorities. On May 7, authorities searched Suu Kyi's residence and later arrested her along with the two long-term houseguests. Suu Kyi was charged with breaking the terms of her house arrest. Suu Kyi was held at the infamous Insein prison for the duration of the trial, which lasted from mid May until August 11. The trial was marred with delays as the regime turned the event into a farcical affair. The defense would only be allotted one witness to testify. The timing of the trial fell during the period in which Suu Kyi's house arrest had been scheduled to expire. International condemnation was widespread. The European Union as well as United Nations Secretary-General Ban Ki-moon and numerous representatives from governments across the world called for the release of Suu Kyi as well as other political prisoners.

The majority of the actual case was heard in July with closing arguments delivered late in the month. The verdict was postponed several times, finally being released on August 11. Suu Kyi was found guilty and sentenced to 18 months of house arrest, while John Yettaw received a seven-year term with hard labor.

In late August 2009, Jim Webb, a U.S. senator from Virginia, arrived in Myanmar to work for the release of John Yettaw. The senator, chairman of the Foreign Relations Committee, was allowed a meeting with Aung San Suu Kyi as well as a diplomatic visit with General Than Shwe. This was the first time that a member of the U.S. government had meet with a leader of Myanmar since the pre-1988 period. Webb was not in Myanmar on behalf of the Obama Administration. The visit was thus unofficial in the context of diplomatic relations. Within days, Yettaw was sentenced to be deported by the authorities; he departed with the senator shortly after. Critics of the regime believed the Webb visit was a mistake. Dealing with the junta could be seen as a sign of acceptance of the repressive antidemocratic policies of the SPDC. Webb viewed the visit strictly as a humanitarian mission, which he hoped could lay the foundation for confidence building in the future.

PROGRESS AND HOPE IN MYANMAR

In May 2008, as part of the process toward what the leadership calls the "road map" to democracy, the dictatorship ratified a new constitution, which led to the first elections in over 20 years. The constitution created a civilian-dominated government, with a two-house parliament that would meet once a year, and an elected head of state. Power remains vested in the commander-in-chief of the armed forces with his military council. With the military controlling a quarter of all seats in parliament, they continue to have a monopoly on decision making.

The Union Solidarity and Development Party (USDP) is the mechanism that the junta works through. The elections were held on November 7, 2010. The results announced later in November showed a 77 percent victory for the ruling USDP. The pre-election playing field was titled heavily in favor of the USDP. Few problems were encountered during the process partially because of the decision of Aung San Suu Kyi's National League for Democracy (NLD) to boycott the process. Even with the overwhelming advantages, the USDP still engaged in massive manipulation of the vote count. The main tool used to control the process was "advance votes." These were ballots that had been distributed early to anyone unable to vote on the allotted day. A huge majority of nearly 80 percent of all legislative seats went to the USDP-backed candidates. Other forms of manipulation and voting irregularities occurred throughout the process.

Once in place, the new regime abolished the SPDC. The military control was guaranteed through the huge majority in parliament as well as the constitutional provisions mentioned earlier. General Thein Sein and 22 of his cabinet ministers switched from military positions to civilian roles shortly before the election of 2010.

With a new system secured, the regime decided to release Aung San Suu Kyi from house arrest on November 13. Two factors may have played into the timing. First, the regime may have felt that Aung San Suu Kyi was a spent force whose time had passed. Second, by releasing her, the regime could put forward a new public face of accommodation, which coincided with the new "civilian" regime.

With her newfound freedom, Aung San Suu Kyi began meetings with NLD leaders to analyze options for the upcoming elections. After several months of internal debate, the NLD decided in late March to boycott the first scheduled elections in 20 years. Because of recent electoral legal changes, the party would be dissolved. This created a rift within the party because if the NLD were to participate in the new process, it would not only abandon its core principles, but also potentially harm its legitimacy. Furthermore the assumption would be that the 1990 victory was invalidated. The party may have also been sending a sign to armed ethnic groups in the northern reaches of the country that the election was illegitimate. The junta was demanding that the ethnic groups disarm.

The actual transfer of power to the new regime took place on March 30, 2011. General Than Shwe retired and was replaced by longtime junta member Thein Sein. The months following the transition saw some of the most significant progress in the history of modern Myanmar. Thein Sein has moved rapidly to begin implementing an ambitious reform agenda first set in his March 2011 inaugural address. Longtime critics of the regime are being consulted and what seems like a sincere attempt at reconciliation is being pushed.

Eventually an approach of cooperation and coordination was implemented between the authorities and Aung San Suu Kyi. This process led to the first in a series of meeting between Suu Kyi and Thein Sein on August 19, 2011. The meeting was held in the new capital of Naypyidaw. This was Aung San Suu Kyi's first visit to the capital. Furthermore, Suu Kyi was invited to attend meetings on the future of the Myanmar economy. The almost unbelievable meetings, subsequent photo opportunities, and state dinner invitations between Thein Sein and the several leading generals and Aung San Suu Kyi stunned international observers. The public nature of the meeting was a radical departure from how earlier negotiations had progressed. Nearly all talks and discussions over the past two decades had taken place in secrecy. Later meetings in 2011 between Aung San Suu Kyi and the Myanmar authorities confirmed that the relationship was vastly different under this new administration. She seems convinced that the new administration is sincere in efforts to move Myanmar forward.

The initial reforms put forward by the regime included legalizing trade unions, the establishment of a human rights commission, and the release of political prisoners, and changes to electoral law. This final change allowed the NLD to once again participate in the political process. The Association of Southeast Asian Nations (ASEAN) is ready to embrace the new regime and will offer Myanmar leadership of the organization for 2014. This decision will be stipulated on the regime continuing on the road to progress on the political front. Economic and political reform will be accelerated, especially as the international community gets on-board to promote progress. The main goals of the president's reform agenda include reinvigorating the economy, reforming national politics, and improving human rights.

The major obstacles to the progress may be resistance from hardliners within the regime and some of the established military bureaucracy, which see reform as a danger to their power base. The inherent weakness of any sort of support base within the country can be a significant obstacle to progress. Decades of isolationism and authoritarianism make change a real challenge to the new regime. Finally, the inherent fragile nature of Myanmar with major rifts along ethnic and religious lines may slow reform initiatives. Efforts to resolve longstanding grievances with several ethnic groups must be a high priority.

THE FUTURE OF MYANMAR

Thein Sein has moved rapidly to begin implementing significant reforms first set out in his March 2011 inaugural address. Opponents of the regime are beginning a dialogue with the administration, as potential breakthroughs are a distinct possibility. Members of the NLD, including Aung San Suu Kyi, have met in Naypyidaw with the leaders of the junta, including Thein Sein. Furthermore, ASEAN, the main regional organization, continues to push for positive change and powers India and China seem to be working to encourage Myanmar to move in a positive direction toward open engagement with the international community.

Thein Sein's inaugural address and the August 2011 speech seem to be opening a new chapter in the history of Myanmar. Critics claim this to be empty rhetoric, but the regime has taken real concrete steps in the direction of openness in both the political and economic realm. The three key areas that are included in the reform agenda include reinvigorating the economy, reforming national politics, and dealing effectively with human rights issues.

The governmental changes that occurred in late March 2011 seemed superficial on the surface. Most members of the new government were at one time tied to the military. President Thein Sein was the prime minister during the previous administration. On a deeper substantive level, the changes seem to be more concrete. Reconciliation with opposition parties and with the ethnic minority groups has taken a high priority.

Following the seminal inaugural address by Thein Sein, plans were underway to begin steps toward change. A key early step was the government assistance in helping to facilitate Aung San Suu Kyi's attendance at Martyrs' Day, the annual celebration honoring her father's role in the independence movement in Myanmar. This was the first time in nearly a decade that she was able to attend. Nearly 3,000 members of the NLD were in attendance for the event. In less than a week after the celebration, Suu Kyi met with Minister Aung Kyi, which culminated in the issuing of a joint statement and a press briefing. Subsequent meetings over the coming weeks confirmed that some accommodation had been ironed out. The joint memorandum spoke of all sides working together for the purpose of national development and focusing on cooperation. Overall, this sense of collaboration and trust that emerged from the meeting indicated a real change in relations between the regime and opposition.

Later in the summer of 2011, Aung San Suu Kyi spoke out openly against government repression of ethnic minorities that was increasing. To the surprise of opposition forces and the international community in general, the regime issued a statement in support of her efforts to work on behalf of resolving the ethnic problem. This change in attitude was considerably different than earlier government pronouncements, which consistently condemned any efforts of Aung San Suu Kyi to speak of matters of a political nature.

An additional breakthrough occurred when Aung San Suu Kyi was invited to Naypyidaw to meet with President Thein Sein. The visit included substantial meetings as well as workshops on economic reform that Suu Kyi attended. During the trip, Suu Kyi was also seated along side key ministers at the state dinner arranged by Sein's wife. This deliberate attempt to show-case the cooperation between Aung San Suu Kyi and the new leadership was obvious. After returning to Yangon, Suu Kyi encouraged fellow democratic advocates and former members of the NLD to believe that real change was on the horizon.

The major breakthrough in Myanmar occurred in November and December of 2011. Aung San Suu Kyi announced that the NLD would rejoin the political process. In addition, the United States moved forward in engaging the regime by sending Secretary of State Hillary Clinton to Myanmar to meet with both the leadership and with opposition leaders, including Aung San Suu Kyi. Clinton became the first U.S. Secretary of State to visit Myanmar since John Foster Dulles in 1955. The series of meetings has set the stage for future dialogue and a hope of engagement with the regime that will lead to democratic progress.

The official announcement by the government in early January 2012 that the NLD and Aung San Suu Kyi would be permitted to run in the 2012 elections was a monumental step forward. Suu Kyi also began to travel again in early 2012. Her popularity had not waned as large crowds gathered at every opportunity to meet "the lady." This decision gave the Myanmar government greater legitimacy both internally and externally. The process culminated in Suu Kyi's decision to run for a seat in the Myanmar parliament in April 2012. Her subsequent election further legitimized the process of reconciliation be-tween the regime and opposition leaders. In addition to Suu Kyi, the NLD won 40 seats in parliament. Even though the NLD's power in parliament is still insignificant, this is the first time they will have a seat at the policymaking table. Statements from the NLD and Aung San Suu Kyi said that further trans-parency in government activities as well as a sincere push to end ethnic strife in Myanmar needed to be high priorities for the regime. Finally, an effort to push for a Panglong type of conference (similar to the one held in 1947) could help iron out differences among the groups still involved in conflict.

In late April, United Nations Secretary-General Ban Ki-moon made a his-toric visit to Myanmar to address the parliament. He was the first foreigner to address the legislature since 1962. The main points emphasized by the secretary-general included the need for international assistance and a new commitment from the global community to engage with the government. Ban Ki-moon held meetings with both Thein Sein and Aung San Suu Kyi.

On May 17, 2012, President Barack Obama announced the easing of an in-vestment ban and the naming of the first U.S. ambassador to Myanmar in 22 years. President Obama's statement said that the moves were a reward for democratic reforms implemented in recent months. Aung San Suu Kyi's election to parliament in April was a major impetus for the decision. Secretary of State Clinton stated that the United States was suspending sanctions on export of American financial services and investment across all sectors of the Myanmar economy. This included the resource-rich lucrative oil, gas, and mining sectors. The final agreement was signed after Clinton held meetings with Myanmar Foreign Minister Wunna Maung Lwin. Clinton stated, "Today we say to American business, invest in Burma, and do it responsibly." Clinton announced that Derek Mitchell, the State Department's coordinator for Burma policy, would be nominated to return to the country as the U.S. ambassador. Part of the U.S. rationale may have been a desire on the part of the U.S. business community not to fall further behind the European community, which was taking similar steps to ease restrictions on trade and investment.

Businesses will still be restricted from having any dealings with the Myanmar military. The framework for sanctions is eroding. The restrictions in place on trade will keep the American export market out of the reach of Myanmar producers. Human rights groups are very cautious about the direction of U.S. policy. The ongoing conflict in the Kachin state has led groups such as "United to End Genocide" and Human Rights Watch to come out somewhat critical of the administration's policy direction. The human rights community believes that by taking such aggressive steps the administration has lost any leverage it had with the Myanmar authorities.

An additional step toward real change was the granting of a passport to Aung San Suu Kyi, which allowed her to travel abroad for the first time in 24 years. Suu Kyi addressed the World Economic Forum in Bangkok, Thailand, on May 31. She cautioned foreign investors against "reckless optimism" in dealing with Myanmar. The fanfare and hype surrounding her first foreign visit was overwhelming.

Suu Kyi's trip abroad did create turmoil back in Myanmar. Critics expressed concern that the trip was poorly planned and managed, with Thai authorities not updated about her itinerary and plans. Furthermore, the trip and comments made at different times to the press by Suu Kyi supposedly angered Thein Sein and may have created a rift in the important relationship. The press in Myanmar criticized Suu Kyi once she returned home from Thailand. Her lack of transparency during the visit as well as controversial visit to Tak province, home to a large population of ethnic minorities on the border between Thailand and Myanmar, was upsetting to the leadership. Thai authorities were concerned that the episode may have strained relations between the two countries. Clear evidence of a potential rift was Thein Sein's decision to cancel his trip to Thailand. He may have been worried about being upstaged by the Suu Kyi's visit, a concern that was of course quite valid.

During the summer of 2012, Suu Kyi visited Europe and spoke at a meeting of the International Labor Organization (ILO) in Geneva, Switzerland.

This stop was followed by the belated acceptance of the Nobel Peace Prize in Oslo, Norway. On June 21, she addressed a joint meeting of the British Parliament, an honor that has been bestowed on few individuals in recent decades. Following her stay in Britain, she traveled to Ireland for a meeting with rock icon Bono. The trip ended with several days in France, where she met with French President Francois Hollande.

Aung San Suu Kyi was submitting works to the Myanmar media. One of the weekly publications, *The Messenger,* ran an interview and cover story about Aung San Suu Kyi. Furthermore, open access to key foreign publications was now available.

It seems apparent that Thein Sein is committed to the changes outlined in his inaugural statement in March 2011. The policy changes have been clearly laid out and a timeline is also in place. Furthermore, the president has also been realistic in his plan, stating the possible obstacles that the regime may need to overcome. Observers within the government as well as outside observers sense a real commitment to change and an eagerness to hear constructive criticism.

Thein Sein had solidified his hold on power, making reform possible. Numerous conservative figures within the previous government were marginalized. It is uncertain whether these individuals were removed from positions, reassigned to other posts within the government, or convinced that change was in the best interest for the future of Myanmar.

Thein Sein's break from Than Shwe's policies was extremely noteworthy. An example of this break has been the restoration of the legacy of Aung San. When the president met with Aung San Suu Kyi he made certain that the photo opportunity took place directly in front of Aung San's portrait in Naypyidaw. Than Shwe felt that by promoting Aung San he would be indirectly helping to legitimize the opposition, including his daughter. The policy of "downgrading" Aung San included taking his photo off of banknotes, deemphasizing the annual Martyrs' Day celebration, and restricting access to his mausoleum. Most experts believe Than Shwe is totally removed from any role in decision making, with dramatically reduced power.

In September of 2012, Aung San Suu Kyi arrived in the United States for a three-week stay. During her visit, Suu Kyi stopped in Washington, D.C., New York, Indiana, Kentucky, Massachusetts, and California. Her most pressing engagements were the stops in Washington, D.C. and New York. During her visit, President Thein Sein was also in the United States for the opening session of the United Nations.

While in Washington, D.C., Suu Kyi was given the Congressional Gold Medal that was awarded in absentia in 2008. She also met with President Barack Obama and congressional leaders. Her trip to Washington, D.C., ended with a speech before a gathering of activists from Amnesty International.

In a sort of homecoming, Suu Kyi returned to New York. She had previously lived there in the 1960s when she worked for the UN. During her visit to the city, she also visited Burmese immigrants and spoke to students at Columbia University and Queens College. Suu Kyi continually stressed the confidence she placed in the new Myanmar leadership and encouraged Western businesses to invest in the country. In all her speeches, Aung San Suu Kyi emphasized the importance of freedom and human rights.

The current administration is actively consulting with Aung San Suu Kyi concerning the steps being taken to restore the public image of her father. His former headquarters are being restored and his mausoleum is being opened for longer periods of time. Some analysts worry that too much of the focus has been placed on the two key individuals: Aung San Suu Kyi and Thein Sein. This concern seems legitimate because the political change has in many ways been a personality-driven process. Neither leader has a clear successor and both have some health concerns, which at some point will create difficulty.

THE LOOMING PROBLEM:
ETHNIC RELATIONS IN MYANMAR

The most pressing concern for the future development of Myanmar both economically and politically is the resolution of the ethnic problem. Issues such as regional autonomy, economic empowerment, sustainable peace, and human rights are all essential if Myanmar is to make progress toward becoming a key regional player in Southeast Asia.

Armed conflict between the government and ethnic minorities has been endemic since independence was granted in the late 1940s. The toll on both combatants and civilians has been enormous. Estimates of over 10,000 deaths per year since independence is noted by Martin Smith in his seminal work *Burma: Insurgency and the Politics of Ethnicity*. In addition to the death toll, the economic devastation, including civilians maimed by landmines, villages destroyed by military operations, and the dislocation of hundreds of thousands has been significant. The social costs, including a burden on health care and education, as well as psychological trauma, are incalculable. With a new administration in place, a unique opportunity to resolve some of these long-standing grievances could be undertaken.

Numerous factors will create challenges for peace initiatives undertaken by any of the parties involved either directly or indirectly. First, several unresolved issues have yet to be addressed by the Myanmar government. Ceasefires have been ironed out on numerous occasions only to be short-lived. This is partially because of a lack of trust as well as a lack of serious concessions on the part of the regime. Several insurgent groups also profit from the illicit narco-criminal undertakings. A final political settlement could undermine these nefarious operations. Most of the insurgents will not disarm, which the government requires if any final resolution is to be agreed upon.

The continuation of multiple armed conflicts with ethnic insurgents also helps to legitimize the need for military rule. It also helps to support the enormous military presence throughout the country. Millions of jobs are based on the military complex, which has been in place for nearly five decades. This gives the military undue political and economic influence throughout Myanmar. Ultimately, this war economy continues to hamper any attempts at legitimate economic gains for the country.

No tangible movement to advance peace and reconciliation between the government and ethnic insurgents has been advocated. This is partially because the government has continually advanced a divide-and-conquer mindset when dealing with ethnic groups. No sort of unity between the numerous ethnic factions has been solidified, which has at times played into the regime's hands. A collaborative effort by the ethnic groups could be beneficial in trying to finalize a lasting settlement.

At times, the ceasefire process seemed to be leading to progress, but most of the time these were short-lived for several reasons. A break in the fighting with the military was usually temporary. A military presence in most ethnic regions continued, which in many cases sparked fighting. Second, the exploitation of natural resources caused increased tension in many of the ethnic areas. The question of who would benefit from the resource extraction was at the root of the escalating tension. This point underlines the core problem of the lack of economic development in most ethnic communities. The tension between the state and ethnic regions has also caused human rights violations to be a persistent problem.

THE KACHIN CASE STUDY

During the early 1960s, the Kachin Independence Organization (KIO) was formed. The masses within the Kachin community tended to push for independence, while the leadership had the more realistic goal of autonomy within a federal system. During the next several decades, alliances were formed and broken between the numerous ethnic groups that had grievances with the military junta. Ceasefires with the regime were commonplace but never long lasting.

Unquestionably, the most serious ethnic problem is the ongoing dispute in the Kachin area. This problem is centered in the Kachin state as well as the northern region of the Shan state. The KIO is the most unified and organized resistance group currently opposing the regime in Myanmar. Earlier ceasefires have failed to lead to any long-term sustainable peace in the region.

During the early 1990s, war weariness had set in, leading to reconciliation with the government. The KIO leadership believed that it was in the best interest of the Kachin people to be included in the national political process. After a series of negotiations throughout the early 1990s, a final ceasefire agreement was signed in February 1994. The agreement included the establishment of a liaison office to ensure open communications; guarantees for peace between the former warring factions; and, finally, emphasis on efforts toward economic development. The KIO participated in the national convention that had started in 1993. The convention would continue to meet sporadically until 2007. As the convention approached closure, the KIO submitted a final proposal, which included 19 points. The authorities did not reply to the KIO request and the issue was never discussed during the ending sessions of the convention.

The Kachins took a stand against the referendum to promulgate the new constitution. Kachin leader Dr. Tu Ja resigned from the KIO and formed a new party, the Kachin State Progressive Party, in order to participate in the electoral process. This was done in order to adhere to the government requirement that prohibited parties desist from having contact with organizations in revolt against the state. In spite of this, the Kachin party was denied permission to participate in the elections. The Kachin leadership was disappointed with the government decision—they felt that over a decade of cooperation was meaningless.

Kachin leaders faced heavy criticism for having been denied electoral participation. Many citizens felt that the Kachin leadership was overly concerned with the extraction of resources from the region rather than making significant political gains. The ceasefire agreement gave the military more of an advantage in dealing with the ethnic communities. Local citizens felt that social and economic cooperation had been an utter failure for the common Kachin citizen. The period of the ceasefire agreement saw a significant increase in drug abuse and HIV / AIDS within the Kachin community.

Hostilities between the KIO and government intensified during 2010 to 2011. The government declared the earlier ceasefire void and took several aggressive steps that were regarded as hostile by the Kachins. The Myanmar authorities decided to implement the following: the closure of several KIO offices, the failure to allow Kachin political parties to register for the elections,

and altering the tone in communications by referring to the members of the
Kachin movement as insurgents.

In early June 2010, the conflict reached an escalation point. Myanmar forces
clashed with KIO forces close to the site of two Chinese-operated hydroelectric dams at Tarpein. Several KIO representatives were captured and killed
and a Kachin outpost was overrun. This lead to the Kachin forces being put
on war alert. Kachin forces destroyed several government instillations and
bridges over the next several days. As hostilities intensified, human rights violations on the part of government forces had become commonplace, according
to Amnesty International and Asia Watch. A report released in December 2011
by Muse detailed atrocities committed during the 2010 to 2011 period. One of
the most devastating parts of the escalation in fighting has been the number
of civilians displaced throughout the region. This not only takes a toll on the
population, but also hinders economic development.

Talks were held with the regime during the summer of 2010, but Kachin
authorities wanted to ensure that any future political agreements regarding
the ethnic question included all of the factions nationwide. This stipulation is
unacceptable to the government, which has used a divide-and-conquer strategy very effectively throughout the past five decades. The Kachin leadership
has requested Chinese assistance in ironing out the diplomatic issues, but thus
far Beijing has refused to get directly involved.

The fighting between the government and KIO forces continued through
2010–2011. Since the Kachins believe that the Myanmar authorities reneged
on earlier agreements, making a lasting agreement is problematic without
guarantees being in place. As the cycle of violence continues, a durable solution becomes difficult. With the new administration of Thein Sein in place, the
Kachin leadership will hopefully realize that the best opportunity for a long-
term solution in recent decades may be possible.

A major step toward reconciliation was taken when the Myanmar authorities announced the suspension of work on the Chinese-built Myitsone dam
project on September 30, 2011. The massive project was the largest of seven
hydroelectric dams being constructed in the Kachin state. The Chinese government had signed on to the project in 2007 with construction starting in
2009. The project was being built by China Power Investment Corporation in
partnership with the Asia World Company of Myanmar and the state-owned
Myanmar Electric Power Enterprise. The dam (with a completion date of
2019) was to be the 15th-largest hydropower station in the world. The problem
from the Kachin perspective was that nearly all of the electricity generated
was to be exported to China's Yunnan province. Furthermore, several rivers
would be flooded by the dam, which ultimately would destroy several historically and culturally important sites significant to the Kachin people. This
in addition to the lack of benefits for any local communities and the massive

displacement that would take place caused significant tension between the Myanmar authorities and Kachin leadership.

With a new leadership in place in 2011, a campaign against the project intensified. A national debate transpired in part because of the easing of media restrictions by the new regime. During the debate, intense nationalism emerged against the project based on the fact that the Irrawaddy River, a symbol of Myanmar, was to be dammed in the project. This was portrayed as tampering with the national heritage of the country. The fact that China was directly involved only served to further fuel the national intensity. The final point of opposition was on environmental grounds. The opposition was massive and organized, which played into the regime's decision to cancel the project. This move on the part of the government is a significant step in easing tension with the Kachin population.

THE ROHINGYA CONTROVERSY

Myanmar's Muslims are mainly Sunni and constitute four percent of the population. They live mostly in the north of Rakhine state (also known as Arakan along the Bangladesh-Myanmar border). The majority are known as Rohingya, and are considered to be of Bengali origin. (An estimated 250,000 Rohingya from Myanmar live in Bangladesh.) They are denied full citizenship in Myanmar, which has sparked considerable controversy in recent years. The authorities claim that the Rohingya are not one of Myanmar's historic ethnic nationalities. Even if this is the case, the Rohingya have undoubtedly lived in Myanmar for several centuries. Their language is derived from the Bengali and is similar to the Chittagonian dialect. An additional group of Muslims in Myanmar are known as the Arakanese or Burmese Muslims. They speak Rakhine, which is closely related to Burmese.

The human rights situation in the Muslim areas of Myanmar has been a grave concern recently. The Muslim minority was targeted for extreme persecution during the reign of Than Shwe. Most of the Muslim minority population is not granted citizenship, barring them from employment and economic opportunities. Travel is restricted, which causes numerous hardships in areas such as education, health care, and employment. In addition, they face extortion and forced labor and serious religious persecution. The destruction of religious sites, including mosques, has been documented. It would be accurate to label the situation regarding the Rohingya as ethnic cleansing.

The army and tatmadaw have been guilty of significant human rights violations in the Muslim areas. Human Rights Watch, Amnesty International, and Doctors without Borders have all documented cases of forced deportation and excessive violence in Rakhine state. Overcrowded camps have been set up to take in the influx of refugees across the border in Bangladesh. Numerous cases of child abduction, rape, forced labor, and kidnapping have been documented by multiple human rights authorities. Medecins Sans Frontieres (Doctors without Borders) claims that violence increased significantly in late 2010. Several doctors treated patients for beatings, machete wounds, and rape. Furthermore, the refugee population was running out of food and drinking water. In addition, the sanitation conditions in the camps have been worsening and subsequently the spread of disease is increasing.

Ethnic tension in Rakhine State was rekindled during June 2012 following a series of events that led to increased sectarian violence. The rape and murder of a Buddhist girl by three Muslim men and the subsequent lynching of nearly a dozen Muslims by a mob of 300 Buddhists initially started the violence. Ultimately, dozens of Rohingyas were killed and hundreds wounded as the violence and tension increased in June. Furthermore, the sectarian violence led to the displacement of more than 30,000 Muslims, and the property loss was in the millions.

Thein Sein called for a State of Emergency in order to quell the violence. The ethnic and religious hostility seems to run high in this region of Myanmar as the Buddhist majority pushes for the forced removal of the Muslim population across the border into Bangladesh. A resolution to this tense situation seems remote.

Resolving the ethnic problem is Myanmar is the single most important issue facing the current government. In many respects, the lack of democratic gains in the modern period and the subsequent militarization of Myanmar stem from the ethnic troubles encountered by earlier regimes. It was the fear of a possible fragmentation that led the authorities to adopt a strong centralized authority dominated by a heavy police and military presence.

CONCLUSION

The international community may be reaching a crossroads in dealing with the military regime in Myanmar. For the past two decades, Western nations have attempted to isolate the regime and possibly institute regime change. These policies have failed miserably. The peasants in Myanmar bore the brunt of the suffering because of the sanctions, trade restrictions, and investment limitations imposed by international actors. With a military option totally out of the question, international policy in dealing with Myanmar is problematic. With no chance of China, India, or the Southeast Asian community taking a hard-line stance against the junta, serious progress seemed unrealistic. However, the positive moves made recently seem irreversible.

One option is to continue the constructive engagement in the hope of enticing reform in Myanmar. The United Nations appointed Ibrahim Gambari to try and facilitate dialogue with the junta. An international consensus must be structured in order to pressure the regime at the appropriate time. Simultaneously, global actors must provide serious incentives to prod the junta to continue the reforms already underway. Only a solid plan to do both can work if change is going to occur. Only time will tell if Aung San Suu Kyi and Thein Sein can successful manage the process that is currently underway. Factions within both the military and democratic opposition are not totally content with the steps that have been taken. Whether these steps are irreversible remains to be seen.

Notable People in
the History of Myanmar

Alaugsithu (1090–1160). Grandson of Kyanzittha and the son of Prince Saw Yin and Princess Shwe Ein Si, Alaugsithu became the fourth king of the Bagan dynasty. Prince Alaugsithu ascended the throne in 1113 at the age of 23 and reigned for 47 years. Alaugsithu spent the early years of his reign suppressing revolts in Tenasserim and Arakan. During his reign he commissioned several pagodas, including Shwegugyi and Thabyinnyu. Alaugsithu was murdered by one of his sons, Narathu, in 1160.

Alaùngpayà (1714–1760). Also known as U Aung Zeya, he was the king and founder of the Konbaung dynasty; he reigned from 1752 to 1760. Originally a headman from the village of Moksobo in the Mu River valley, Alaùngpayà rose to prominence as a resistance leader against Mon rule. He was crowned king at Moksobo following the capture of several Mon cities in 1752. Alaùngpayà defeated the Mon following the capture of Ava in 1753 and Pegu in 1757. Following his victory over the Mon, Alaùngpayà devoted himself to the administrative and military reorganization of Burma. Alaùngpayà was mortally wounded in his last campaign against Siam in April 1760 and died returning to Burma.

Anaukhpetlun (1578–1628). He was the grandson of King Bayinnaung and the sixth king of the Toungoo dynasty; he reigned from 1606 to 1628.

Anaukhpetlun inherited the kingdom of Ava and the Shan states. Following his installation he set about restoring the Burmese kingdom. During his reign he pursued a series of military campaigns against the kingdom of Prome, Martaban, Tavoy, Tenasserim, and Lan Na, eventually unifying the Burmese kingdom. In 1617, he made Pegu the capital and crowned himself the king of Pegu later that year. He was murdered by his son Minyedaikpya in 1628.

Anawrahta Min Saw (1014–1077). Also known as Aniruddha, he was the founder and first king (r. ca. 1044–1077) of the Bagan dynasty. He was the first ruler to unify both Upper Burma and Lower Burma and extended Burmese suzerainty over neighboring Shan states and Arakan. Between 1057 and 1059 Anawrahta led his army to the kingdom of Nan-Chou in search of the Buddha's tooth relic. During his reign Anawrahta transformed Bagan into the religious and cultural center of Southeast Asia. He converted to Therāvāda Buddhism and made it the state religion of Bagan. Anawrahta built numerous pagodas during his reign. He also established contact with Ceylon and received a copy of the complete Tripitaka, which was placed in the Shwedagon pagoda in Bagan.

Aung Gyi (1919–). As a soldier in the Fourth Burma Rifles, he rose to the rank of brigadier general and was member of the Revolutionary Council. Aung Gyi became an outspoken critic of the government of Ne Win during the August 8, 1988, uprising.

Aung Gyi rose to prominence as the leading military administrator in the caretaker government of 1958–1960, coconspirator in the coup d'état of March 2, 1962, and member of the following Revolutionary Council. Forced to resign from the Revolutionary Council, Aung Gyi was imprisoned from 1965 to 1968 and then again from 1973 to 1974. Following his later release, he returned to private life. He was imprisoned again in 1988 following the publication of four open letters to Ne Win in which he criticized the "Burmese Way to Socialism" and warned of social unrest in Myanmar. He joined the Aung-Suu-Tin coalition and became president of the National League for Democracy (NLD) following the State Law and Order Restoration Council's (SLORC) seizure of power on September 18, 1988. He later resigned from the NLD on December 3, 1988, to form the Union Nationals Democracy Party.

Aung `Kyi (1946–). He is a retired major general of the Myanmar Army, and is currently the minister of labor and holds a concurrent appointment minister of social welfare, relief and settlement in the government of Myanmar. He graduated from the Officers Training School and went on to serve as deputy minister for labor in November 2006. He was appointed minister of labor in October 2007. Aung Kyi was appointed as SPDC's official liaison to Aung San Suu Kyi.

Aung San (1915–1947). Also known as Bo Te Za, he was the founder of the modern Burmese military and a leading political figure of the Burmese independence movement from 1935 to 1947. He is also considered the architect of the Union of Burma.

Aung San was born on February 13, 1915, in Natmouk, Magwe district in central Burma. His first involvement in politics was as a leader of the students strike at Rangoon University in 1936. He was elected president of the All Burma Students' Union from 1936 to 1938. In 1938, Aung San joined the Do Bama Asi Ayon students association and served as its secretary-general until 1940. He was also one of the Thirty Comrades who was sent by Do Bama Asi Ayon to receive Japanese military instruction before returning with the invading Japanese as the head of the Burmese Independence Army (BIA) in 1941. Aung San served as minister of defense from 1943 to 1945 in Ba Maw's newly proclaimed "independent" government. Cofounder of the Anti-Fascist People's Freedom League, he would later become deputy chairman of the executive council in 1946. Aung San was assassinated on July 19, 1947, in the council chamber in Rangoon.

Aung San Suu Kyi, Daw (1945–). She is the daughter of Burmese independence hero Aung San. She is the symbol of the Burmese democratic opposition and general secretary of the NLD. She rose to prominence as a leader of the democratic opposition during the 1988 Burmese Spring.

Aung San Suu Kyi was born on June 19, 1945 and was educated in Burma, India, and the United Kingdom. After living and working in Japan and Bhutan she went to Britain to raise her children. She returned to Burma in 1988 for family reasons and became involved in the Burmese democratic movement. Aung San Suu Kyi helped cofound the NLD on September 24, 1988. She spent most of the last two decades under house arrest for her efforts to bring democracy to Myanmar. On April 1, 2012, she stood and won the seat in the Kawhmu constituency in a parliamentary by-election. Aung San Suu Kyi has won numerous international awards, including the Nobel Peace Prize, the Sakharov Prize from the European Parliament, and the U.S. Presidential Medal of Freedom.

Ba Maw (1893–1977). A Burmese political leader active from the early 1930s until 1945, and who rose to prominence as the defense lawyer for rebel leader Saya San. He went on to become an outspoken advocate of Burmese independence. Founder of the Sinyetha Party, Ba Maw was elected to parliament in 1936 and served as premier of Burma from 1937 to 1939. He was imprisoned from 1940 to 1942 by the British. During the Japanese occupation of Burma Ba Maw was the head of the Burmese provisional administration. In 1945, he fled to Japan, where he was captured by the American occupation authorities. He was tried and imprisoned during 1945 to 1946. Following his release he returned to Burma. He was again imprisoned during the rule of General Ne Win.

Bagyidaw (1784–1846). Also known as Maung Sein, he was the grandson of King Bodawpaya and the seventh king of the Konbaung dynasty; he reigned from 1819 until his abdication in 1837. He was made the general of the Northern and Southern Corps of the Royal Cavalry at the age of nine by his grandfather. At the age of 18 he married Princess Hsinbyume, who was the granddaughter of Bodawpaya. His reign saw the first Anglo-Burmese war (1824–1826) that culminated in the Treaty of Yandabo in which the Burmese ceded all of Bodawpaya's western territorial acquisitions and Tenasserim to the British, and pay a large indemnity. His brother Crown Prince Tharrawaddy forced Bagyidaw to abdicate the throne in April 1837.

Binnya Dala (??–1774). He was the last king of the Mon-speaking Restored kingdom of Hanthawaddy; he reigned from 1747 to 1757. Binnya Dala was a key leader in the revolt against the Toungoo dynasty. He succeeded Smim Htaw Buddhaketi following the latter's abdication in 1747. In 1752, he launched an invasion of Upper Burma in which he captured the capital of the Toungoo dynasty, Ava. In 1757, Pegu fell to Alaùngpayà, ending the Restored kingdom of Hanthawaddy. Alaùngpayà's son Hsinbyushin executed Binnya Dala in 1774.

Bodawpaya (1745–1819). He was also known as Bodaw U Waing and was the fourth son of Alaùngpayà, the founder of the dynasty, and the sixth king of the Konbaung dynasty; he reigned from 1782 to 1819. In 1783, he moved the capital from Inwa to Amarapura. The following year he invaded and annexed Arakan, making Arakan a province of Burma. Bodawpaya's oppressive rule in Arakan led to rebellion and his pursuit of rebels into British-controlled Bengal brought him into conflict with the British. In addition, his military campaigns into Assam heightened tensions with the British. He was also a fervent Buddhist who proclaimed himself *Arimittya*, the messianic Buddha destined to conquer the world.

Dhammazedi (1412–1492). He was the 16th king of Hanthawaddy Pegu; he reigned from 1472 to 1492. He is considered one of the most enlightened rulers in Burmese history. A former Buddhist monk, Dhammazedi became the de facto ruler following Queen Shinsawbu relinquishing monarchical duties. Dhammazedi unified and purified Theravāda Buddhism in Pegu. In addition, he was responsible for establishing links with Ceylon.

Min Bin (??–??). He was also known as Ma Pa and was the 12th king of the Mrauk-U dynasty; he ruled from 1531 to 1553. During his reign Arakan reached the height of its power. He forged ties with the Portuguese that enabled Mrauk-U to extend suzerainty over eastern Bengal and defeat an invasion by the Burmese King Tabinshweti.

Min Ko Naing (1962–). Nom de guerre of Paw Oo Tun, he was one of the most prominent student leaders in the pro-democracy uprising of 1988. A third-year university student at the Rangoon Arts and Science University, Min Ko Naing rose to prominence as an advocate for human rights in Burma during the student-led demonstrations. In March 1989, he was arrested and sentenced to 20 years imprisonment for his role in the pro-democracy movement. On November 19, 2004, Min Ko Naing was released from prison, after being imprisoned for 15 years. Following his release from prison, he helped found the 88-generation students' group, which continued to fight for democracy in Burma. He was arrested on August 21, 2007, with other 13 leaders of the 88-generation students for organizing peaceful demonstrations and was sentenced to 65 years imprisonment for his role in the August 2007 demonstrations. Min Ko Naing was released along with numerous other activists on January 13, 2012, as part of a mass presidential pardon for political activists.

Mindon Min (1808–1878). Known as a modernizer, Mindon Min was the last ruler of the Konbaung dynasty, ruling from 1853 to 1878. He ascended the throne following the abdication of his half brother Pagan Min in February 1853. Upon his ascension Mindon Min sued for peace end the second Anglo-Burmese war. He found the last royal capital, Mandalay, in 1757. During his reign Mindon Min undertook a modernization of the administration of government through a series of bureaucratic reforms.

Min-gyi-nyo (1459–1531). He was the founder of the Toungoo dynasty; he reigned from 1486 to 1531. During the early 1490s, Min-gyi-nyo built a new capital and established himself as a military commander. He attacked settlements along the frontier between Ava and Toungoo. He also reigned he conquered the Mohnyin Shan kingdom in northern Burma. In 1510, Min-gyi-nyo founded the first Toungoo dynasty at Toungoo. He died in 1531.

Ne Win (1911–2002). He was also known as Thakin Shu Maung, and was the general and leader of Burma from 1962 to 1988. Ne Win joined the Burmese independence movement Do Bama Asi Ayon in the 1930s. He was one of the Thirty Comrades who was trained by the Japanese; he returned with the invading Japanese as the head of the BIA in 1941. He became commander of the renamed Burma Defense Army in 1943. Following World War II, Ne Win joined the regular army where he rose through the ranks. He was promoted as brigadier general in 1948. In February 1949, he became commander of the armed forces. In 1962, Ne Win ousted the popularly elected Prime Minister U Nu. In

2002, Ne Win was placed under house arrest following the imprisonment of his perceived rivals and remained under house arrest until his death.

Tabinshweti (1512–1550). He was the Toungoo dynasty king who unified Burma during his reign from 1531 to 1550. Tabinshweti led military campaigns against the kingdom of Pegu in 1535 and Martaban and Moulmein in 1541 that ended with Toungoo dominating Lower Burma. Following the unification of Burma, Tabinshweti attempted two unsuccessful campaigns against Tavoy and Ayutthaya, the Siamese capital, in 1548, only to be forced to return to Pegu. Humiliated by the crushing defeats Tabinshweti retreated from public life before being assassinated by a close Mon advisor Smim Sawhtut in 1550, who proclaimed himself king. Tabinshweti's brother-in-law Bayinnaung crushed the Mon revolt and carried on Tabinshweti's work of unifying Burma.

Than Shwe (1933–). He was a general who was a political leader and chairman of the State Peace and Development Council (SPDC) from 1992 to 2011. Shwe resigned his position as chairman of the SPDC in favor of his handpicked successor, Thein Sein. Little is known about his childhood. He was born on February 2, 1933, in Minzo in the Mandalay division. He attended Government High School in Kyaukse. Following high school, Than enlisted in the Burmese Army and was accepted into the Army Officer Training School.

Thibaw Min (1858–1916). Also known as Maung Pu. He was the last king of the Konbaung dynasty, whose reign (1878–1885) ended with the British annexing Upper Burma. The British deposed Thibaw and Upper Burma was incorporated in British India. A younger son of King Mindon Thibaw succeeded his father following a bloody succession massacre orchestrated by his wife, Supayalat. Faced with the prospect of mounting British pressure Thibaw entered into diplomatic negotiations with the French, culminating with a commercial treaty signed in Paris in 1885. A proclamation issued by Thibaw served as a pretext to invade Mandalay and force the unconditional surrender of Thibaw.

U Thant (1909–1974). Also known as Pantanow, U Thant is best known as the third secretary-general of the United Nations; he served from November 30, 1961, to December 31, 1971. He was chosen secretary-general following the death of Dag Hammarskjold in an air crash in the Congo. Prior to his appointment as secretary-general, U-Thant was a civil servant in the newly independent Burma.

U Thant was appointed as director of broadcasting in 1947 and then as the secretary to the government of Burma in the Ministry of Information the following year. He was appointed the secretary for projects in the Office of the Prime Minister in 1953. From 1957 to 1961, U Thant was Burma's Permanent Representative to the United Nations, with the rank of ambassador. In 1959,

he served as one of the vice presidents of the Assembly's 14th session. In 1961, U Thant was chairman of the United Nations Congo Reconciliation Commission. He was appointed as acting secretary-general on November 3, 1961, by the General Assembly. U Thant was unanimously appointed secretary-general by the General Assembly on November 30, 1962. He was reappointed for a second term as secretary-general by the General Assembly on December 2, 1966. His term of office ended on December 31, 1971.

Wareru (1252–1307). Also called Mogado, he was the king of Hanthawaddy Pegu who ruled over Burma from 1287 to 1296. Wareru was a Shan chief who married a daughter of the King Ramkhamhaeng of Sukhotai who managed to become ruler of Martaban in 1281. Following the Mongol sacking of Bagan in 1287, Wareru and the Mon prince of Hanthawaddy Pegu, Tarabya, pushed the Burman back to Upper Burma. Once in control of Lower Burma, Wareru had Tarabya assassinated and declared himself king.

Yan Naing, Bo (1918–1989). Nom de guerre of Tun Shein Ko, he was one of the "Thirty Comrades" and son-in-law of Ba Maw. Yan Naing was active in prewar student movement. He rose to prominence as the commander of the BIA fighting the British at the battle of Shwedaung in 1942. Following World War II Yan Naing was involved in politics. He joined the U-Nu's exiled Parliamentary Democracy Party in 1969 and became one of the commanders of the Patriotic Liberation Army. He returned to Burma in the 1980 amnesty.

Bibliographic Essay

Recent research on Myanmar suffers from the closed political environment in the country. Travel to the region for researchers has been problematic for several decades. Primary accounts of life in modern Myanmar are written covertly, and either smuggled out or written under pseudonyms. Most research on the country has come from secondary sources from journalists, and Western academics.

Many of the early contributions to postindependence Burma are general compilations on Southeast Asia generally. John Cady's *Postwar Southeast Asia*, D.G.E. Hall's *A History of South East Asia*, and David Steinberg's *In Search of Southeast Asia* are comparative works on the region that included significant contributions on the early postindependence period. Cady's early works on Burma including *A History of Modern Burma*, set the mark for scholarship on Burmese studies.

On the postcolonial independence period Hugh Tinker's *The Union of Burma: A Study of the First Years of Independence* was the earliest account of the fledging independent Burma. Frank Trager's *Building a Welfare State in Burma, 1948–1956* discusses the failed attempt at state building following the departure of the British and the assassination of Aung San. Political scientist Robert Taylor's *The State in Burma* (1987) and the updated *The State of Myanmar* (2009) are exhaustive overviews that chronicle the evolution and development of the

modern Burmese state. Thant Myint-U's *The Making of Modern Burma* written by U Thant's grandson is a readable resource that mixes both primary and secondary accounts.

The defining scholarship on the developments in modern Burmese comes from Georgetown University political scientist David Steinberg. *Burma: The State of Myanmar* and *Turmoil in Burma: Contested Legitimacies in Myanmar* are two of the most significant scholarly works on contemporary Burma. Steinberg is able to analyze the historical development as well as the political changes within Burmese society. More recently, Michael Charney from the London School of Economics and Politics has completed a very concise and readable history of contemporary Burma. His *A History of Modern Burma* covers the Burma from the late colonial stage through the Saffron Revolution of 2007. This very organized and fluid work is a must read for anyone interested in developments in modern Burma.

Mary Callahan's *Making Enemies: War and State Building in Burma* is a significant contribution in the field of military influence in Burmese politics and development. Josef Silverstein's *Military Rule and the Politics of Stagnation* is an additional work of serious scholarship on civil-military relations in Myanmar. Callahan and Silverstein are the definitive experts on the dominating role of the military in Burmese society. Monique Skidmore's *Karaoke Fascism* is a fascinating look at the oppression of military rule in Burma.

Martin Smith in *Burma: Insurgency and the Politics of Ethnicity* best explains the complicated role of minorities in Burmese society. Additionally Bertil Linter's works on ethnic politics specifically the problems with the Shan minority are chronicled in *Contemporary Southeast Asia*. Carolyn Wakeman and San San Tin's *No Time for Dreams Living in Burma Under Military Rule* is one of the newest additions to of dissident writers who have fled Burma in recent years. The issues of human rights violations and mistreatment of minority populations are discussed in the numerous reports from Amnesty International and Human Rights Watch, Burma. Furthermore a plethora of advocacy groups devoted to furthering the cause of Burmese democracy have formed over the past two decades. The most noteworthy organizations include the U.S. Campaign for Burma, Burma Watch, Burma Campaign UK, and the Free Burma Rangers.

Travel works on Burma are some of the most helpful books in order to gain a general understanding of life in modern Burma. Emma Larkin's masterfully written *Finding George Orwell in Burma* follows the writer's footsteps from his time as a police officer in colonial Burma. Larkin brings to life the common Burmese peasant and explains the relationship between citizen and state under the harsh conditions of authoritarianism. The *Myanmar (Burma)* travel guide from the *Lonely Planet* series written by Robert Reid and Michael Grosberg does a through job with geography and travel highlights for the potential visitor to the region.

Books on or about Nobel Prize–winning pro-democracy leader Aung San Suu Kyi are abundant. Her earlier work *Freedom from Fear* is a compilation of early writings completed prior to her incarceration as well as later more politically charged pieces dealing with the struggle for democracy in Burma. Alan Clements's *The Voice of Hope* includes a series of interviews with Aung San Suu Kyi conducted in 1995–1996 after her first release from house arrest. This insightful look at Suu Kyi helps the reader gain a working knowledge of how she deals with the struggle against the junta.

The repressive nature of the military junta is Myanmar is chronicled in the numerous Human Rights Watch and Amnesty International reports. The brutal crackdown against the monks in the fall of 2007 is thoroughly documented in the human rights reports from both organizations. Furthermore the human rights community details the lack of action by the regime in the post-Nargis recovery efforts in 2008.

Index

About the Authors

WILLIAM J. TOPICH is chair of the Department of Social Science at Pulaski Academy, a college preparatory school in Little Rock, Arkansas. He is also adjunct professor in the Department of Political Science at the University of Arkansas at Little Rock. His courses include politics of developing areas, world cultures, and global issues. Topich is a contributor to Greenwood's *The Vietnam War: Handbook of the Literature and Research.* Topich has conducted research in Cambodia in the late 1990s and most recently in Pakistan during 2010.

KEITH A. LEITICH teaches political science in the Division of Business and Social Science at Pierce College Puyallup, Puyallup, Washington. He has previously taught at North Seattle Community College and Arkansas State University. Leitich is a contributor to ABC-CLIO's *The 9/11 Encyclopedia: Second Edition*; *The Encyclopedia of Middle East Wars: The United States in the Persian Gulf, Afghanistan, and Iraq Conflicts*; and *The Greenwood Dictionary of Education: Second Edition.* He has contributed articles to *History of Northern Buddhism* and *Geopolitics of Central Asia in the Post-Cold War Era: A Systemic Analysis,* and has been published in several journals, including Asian studies publications.

Other Titles in the Greenwood Histories of the Modern Nations
Frank W. Thackeray and John E. Findling, Series Editors

The History of Afghanistan
Meredith L. Runion

The History of Argentina
Daniel K. Lewis

The History of Australia
Frank G. Clarke

The History of the Baltic States
Kevin O'Connor

The History of Brazil
Robert M. Levine

The History of Bulgaria
Frederick B. Chary

The History of Cambodia
Justin Corfield

The History of Canada
Scott W. See

The History of Central America
Thomas Pearcy

The History of the Central Asian
Republics
Peter L. Roudik

The History of Chile
John L. Rector

The History of China, Second Edition
David C. Wright

The History of Congo
Didier Gondola

The History of Costa Rica
Monica A. Rankin

The History of Cuba
Clifford L. Staten

The History of the Czech Republic
and Slovakia
William M. Mahoney

The History of Ecuador
George Lauderbaugh

The History of Egypt
Glenn E. Perry

The History of El Salvador
Christopher M. White

The History of Ethiopia
Saheed Adejumobi

The History of Finland
Jason Lavery

The History of France
W. Scott Haine

The History of Germany
Eleanor L. Turk

The History of Ghana
Roger S. Gocking

The History of Great Britain
Anne Baltz Rodrick

The History of Greece
Elaine Thomopoulos

The History of Haiti
Steeve Coupeau

The History of Holland
Mark T. Hooker